Ralph Brookfield

Ralph Brookfield trained as a molecular physicist, worked as a copy editor, software engineer, and freelance writer, ran his own software business, then became an award-winning director of technology in the digital television industry.

Since 2012, he has pursued his passions as a tutor, writer, and amateur musician. He is married, has two grown-up children, and is a founder member of the infamous Hanwell Ukulele Group in West London.

First published in the UK in 2022 by SUPERNOVA BOOKS
67 Grove Avenue, Twickenham, TW1 4HX

Supernova Books is an imprint of Aurora Metro
www.aurorametro.com @aurorametro FB/AuroraMetroBooks

Editor: Cheryl Robson

Production: Charlotte Banks

We gratefully acknowledge financial assistance from the National Lottery Heritage Fund, UK.

Images: Mike Peters, Dave Peabody, CC, flickr, wikimedia, contributors' own images, stock shots

Printed in the UK by Short Run Press, Exeter, UK.

ISBNs: 978-1-913641-22-1 (print version)
978-1-913641-23-8 (ebook version)

Made possible with
Heritage Fund

ROCK'S DIAMOND YEAR

Celebrating London's Music Heritage

Introduced by
RALPH BROOKFIELD

SUPERNOVA BOOKS

Dedicated to the memory of Don Craine

The Downliners Sect, c. 1964
L-R: Terry Gibson, Ray Stone, Don Craine, Keith Grant, Johnny Sutton

CONTENTS

INTRODUCTION   9
Ralph Brookfield
THE EALING CLUB   24
Alistair Young
AN ADOLESCENCE IN MUSIC   40
Robert Hokum
THE EEL PIE ISLAND HOTEL & EEL PIE CLUB   56
Gina Way
THE CRAWDADDY CLUB   68
David Sinclair
IGNITION – GIORGIO GOMELSKY   84
Cheryl Robson
THE BULL'S HEAD   94
Pete Feenstra
THE HALF MOON   102
Patrick Humphries
GETTING ON DOWN TO RICKY-TICK CLUBS   110
Pete Clack
THE MARQUEE   124
Charlotte Banks
THE 100 CLUB   138
Richard Luck
BIOGRAPHIES   146

Ben Waters (piano), Steve King (bass guitar), Tom Waters (sax), Terry Marshall
taken at the former premises of The

tewart (harmonica/percussion), Robert Hokum (guitar), Paul White (drums).
s Club, 2016. Photo: Wendy Auld

Dancers at the Eel Pie Island Hotel, c. 1962. Photo: Mike Peters

INTRODUCTION

Ralph Brookfield

*"Everyone talks about rock these days;
the problem is they forget about the roll."*
– Keith Richards

In his autobiography *Life* Keith Richards quotes part of a letter he wrote to his Aunt Patty in 1962:

> "The Saturday after Mick and I are taking 2 girls over to our favourite Rhythm & Blues club over in Ealing, Middlesex. They got a guy on electric harmonica Cyril Davies fabulous always half-drunk unshaven plays like a mad man, marvellous.[i.i]"

'The Saturday after' was Saturday 7th April 1962. That evening, young Richards and his fledgling bandmate Jagger were impressed by the slide guitar performance of one 'Elmo Lewis' (aka Brian Jones) cranking out his hero Elmore James' *Dust my Broom* on the tiny stage of Alexis Korner's 'Rhythm & Blues Club No. 1', a damp basement opposite Ealing Broadway Station. Jones was a new guest performer with Korner's house band, stepping up as a featured artist when pugnacious frontman Davies paused for a pint. It was a date that came to mark the conception of British rock music.

Rock's Diamond Year celebrates the 60th anniversary of the birth of British electric blues in Ealing, the 'Queen' of the

---

i. i   Richards, Keith (2010) *Life*, Orion Publishing, ISBN10 0753826615, p79

London suburbs. Korner and Davies' new club opened in March 1962, and led to a revival of Chicago blues by teenagers centred around South West London, intent on copying Black music. British pop/rock music was dominant in the *Billboard 100* from the arrival of the Beatles in 1963 until US artists repossessed the genre in the late 1970s.

The history of the Ealing Club is detailed by the club's current director Alistair Young in his chapter. The first encounter there of Brian Jones, Mick Jagger, and Keith Richards in April 1962 was such a significant event because it brought together three young musicians from the nascent British rhythm and blues scene who were turned on both by the gritty electric blues of Muddy Waters and Elmore James – as reproduced by Korner's and Davies' Blues Incorporated – and by rock 'n' rollers like Little Richard, Chuck Berry, Elvis Presley, and Buddy Holly. Many of their contemporaries from the UK R&B scene at the time would have dismissed Berry, Elvis, and Buddy as "pop", if they gave them any listening time at all. But the amalgam that Jones, Richards, and Jagger created was irresistible to young suburban Londoners seeking rebellious adventure through music to dance to that made their parents, and even older brothers and sisters, deeply uncomfortable.

The "Rollin' Stones" made their debut at the Marquee Club in Soho in July 1962. They spent the coldest winter in living memory (62/63) warming the cockles of West London youth at the Ealing Club (with occasional gigs at other London venues). Later in this book David Sinclair adroitly recounts how by April 1963, they had assembled the powerhouse of Ian Stewart (piano), Bill Wyman (bass), and Charlie Watts (drums), and had all but grown out of a residency at Giorgio Gomelsky's Crawdaddy Club in the Station Hotel Richmond[ii]. An image makeover, UK tour, and recording contract with Decca was to follow in very short order, under the mercurial management

---

i. ii   May, Barry (1963) *Richmond and Twickenham Times* 13 April

of 19-year-old Andrew Loog Oldham and his business partner Eric Easton. By February 1964 the Stones were up there with the Beatles in the UK charts...

The popularity of the Stones' music with suburban teens helped other South West London bands to follow in their footsteps. The Detours, a tough band led by Shepherd's Bush 'face' Roger Daltrey had been playing pubs, clubs, and hotels around Acton, Ealing, Greenford, and Hanwell for a couple of years before the Stones came together at the Ealing Club. By the end of 1963, promoter Robert Druce was able to book them as support for well-known acts in bigger venues, including a gig opening for the Stones at Putney Town Hall on 22 December[iii]. The following year contractual issues forced Daltrey to rename his band The Who – a suggestion from bandmate Pete Townshend.

The Stones' Crawdaddy Club residency was taken over by a band from Kingston, Surrey called the Yardbirds, featuring a young guitar player called Eric Clapton[iv]. An early jamming mate of Clapton's from the Kingston days was Isleworth-born guitarist David Brock, later the founder and perennial member of space-rockers Hawkwind.

When Jagger and Richards visited the Ealing Club in April '62 they were part of a college band called Little Boy Blue and the Blue Boys, with Keith's fellow Sidcup Art college student Dick Taylor on guitar. Taylor joined the Rollin' Stones briefly on bass, but with the arrival of Bill Wyman and his more 'professional' stage rig, he left to form his own band with fellow Sidcup student Phil May on harmonica and vocals. The Pretty Things, named for a Willie Dixon number, stuck to raw rhythm and blues for several years without achieving huge commercial success, but enjoyed periods of popularity in the late 60s with psychedelic album *SF Sorrow* and glam offerings

i. iii   Neill, Andrew; Kent, Matthew (2009). *Anyway Anyhow Anywhere: The Complete Chronicle of The Who 1958–1978.* Sterling Publishing. ISBN 978-0-7535-1217-3.

i. iv   http://earlyblues.org/british-blues-early-british-blues-clubs-crawdaddy-club/

Silk Torpedo and *Savage Eye*. Support came from Yardbird-to-Zeppelin London guitarist Jimmy Page and Zeppelin's Swansong label. Page archivist Adrian T'Vell commented:

"When Andrew Oldham fed the press with the line 'Would you let your daughter go out with a Rolling Stone?' the majority of parents said 'No,' but the Pretty Things... parents wouldn't let their daughters within a mile of them. Wilder than the Stones, their Garage/R&B sound invented 60s punk[v]."

Singer Arthur (Art) Wood (elder brother of Ronnie Wood who would later join the Stones) was another regular with Korner's Blues Incorporated at the Ealing Club. In 1962 Wood formed the Artwoods, with Jon Lord on keyboards and Keef Hartley (drums). The Artwoods were regulars at the iconic Eel Pie Island Club 1963-68, subject of a chapter in this book by the Eel Pie Club's current owner Gina Way. In 1968 former Artwoods member Jon Lord would help to found original monsters of heavy rock Deep Purple, who rehearsed in the nearby Hanwell Community Centre.

The Artwoods, 1967

i. v   T'Vell, Adrian (1995) https://jppsessionman.jimdofree.com/the-pretty-things/

INTRODUCTION

Hanwell lies a mile or so down the Uxbridge road from the Ealing club. Popular with musicians and entertainers since the days of music hall because of its low rents and proximity to central London by rail, it became the site for two formative venues for British rock.

Drummer Jim Marshall, the 'father of loud' was born in nearby Southall. In 1960 he opened his first music shop J & T Marshall, at 76 Uxbridge Road (now a gent's hairdressers). The 'T' standing for Jim's son, saxophonist Terry Marshall, who still grooves regularly in West London bands. The shop branched out from drums and instruments and into bigger premises at 93 Uxbridge Road after the 1962 launch of Marshalls' first guitar amplifier, which as Alistair Young relates, had an important debut at the Ealing Club. Marshall's shops became a popular hangout for London bands seeking powerful stage amplification. In 1966 Hanwell drummer Mitch Mitchell brought his new bandmate Jimi Hendrix to the Marshall shop to check out the latest gear. Thereafter, Hendrix seldom used other stage rigs. In 2013 the Hanwell Hootie music festival, sponsored by Marshall Amplification, unveiled a plaque on a nearby building to commemorate Jim Marshall's lifelong contribution to rock music.

Hanwell Community Centre was a popular rehearsal venue for a generation of 'loud' bands that grew out of the British R&B boom. Formerly the Central London District Schools, which provided shelter and education to the young Charlie Chaplin, the vast Victorian building occupies an isolated hillside site. Its basement now houses a new club (The Hanwell Cavern) with a truly authentic atmosphere dedicated to live music inspired by the 1960s London R&B explosion. The Hanwell Community Centre Consortium quote The Who, Deep Purple, Procul Harum, Led Zeppelin, Uriah Heep, Gene Vincent, The Animals, and Jerry Lee Lewis amongst the famous musical names who have used the building.[vi]

i. vi   https://www.facebook.com/pages/category/Nonprofit-Organization/
Hanwell-Community-Centre-Consortium-Ltd-1671939559714104/

The Goldhawk Club

Virtually none of the original sites key to the West London R&B boom still operate as music venues. Even the Ealing Club only opens its doors to live music lovers for the occasional commemorative event. In 2012, the fiftieth anniversary of the founding of Alexis Korner's 'Rhythm and Blues Club Number 1' was commemorated by a group of enthusiasts and musicians including Terry Marshall and the late (not 'Sir')[vii] Charlie Watts with a blue plaque. Most weekends it is a nightclub, with dancing to recorded music.

The Station Hotel, Richmond, home to the original Crawdaddy Club, is currently a restaurant, but features a fortnightly jazz club called 'Off the Rails' which opened in September 2021. The Oldfield Tavern Greenford, where The Who played habitually, was demolished in the early 2000s to be replaced by a block of flats. The Feathers Hotel, nearly opposite the Ealing Club, also a Who venue, is now a bank. The Goldhawk Club in Shepherd's Bush *(above)* remains today a traditional social club, sporting a blue plaque commemorating The Who's appearances there 1963-65. The Eel Pie Island

---

i. vii Watts famously opined that knighthood honours would be the 'death of the Rolling Stones' https://www.express.co.uk/celebrity-news/1481698/charlie-watts-royal-snub-knighthoods-would-be-death-of-rolling-stones

Hotel site is now home to a waterside residential development of townhouses. Eel Pie Island remains a magical place to visit – perhaps not quite as it was for the young Gina Way in 1963, but still a haven of mystery and quirkiness across the footbridge from Twickenham's suburban charms.

In his book *As You Were*, National Service "virgin soldier" John Mansfield recalls his first visit to Eel Pie Island while on leave in 1957. Once demobbed, Mansfield and his great friend Philip Hayward started a series of clubs they called Ricky-Tick after the ragtime jazz rhythm that was the latest youth craze in late-1950s suburban London. But the name also conveyed the urgency of the new UK teenage music, rhythm and blues, through its US military slang meaning: 'quick'. Our chapter by Pete Clack documents the many incarnations and personal recollections of the Ricky-Tick. Its spiritual home was Clewer Mead, a crumbling great house now buried under the Windsor Leisure Centre, but Mansfield and Hayward first booked the Rolling Stones at the original Ricky-Tick venue, the Star and Garter, 133 Peascod St Windsor[viii] on 14 December 1962. From 1963, the Ricky-Tick became a brand of pilgrimage for young R&B fans. Its posters featured the iconic primitive screen print graphics of band leader Hogsnort Rupert, aka Bob McGrath.

Mansfield describes his early marketing policy, inviting *au pairs* and nursing students, who made the clubs a magnet for 'every red-blooded young man in the neighbourhood'. He had noticed the remarkable effect of the Rolling Stones on the young women in the audience: "By the time they'd finished their first number you could tell that they'd hit the girls' musical G-spot because they were all just

i. viii   also now demolished

screaming wild. … hypnotic music … a fusion between Bo Diddley and Chuck Berry …all pulsating rhythms.[ix]" Later in this book, Pete Clack documents the expansion of Mansfield and Hayward's roster in the years that followed, to include stars from the USA such as Geno Washington and the Supremes, as well as UK bands that became household names such as Pink Floyd. Those performances in clubs around the southwestern hinterlands of London were to play a large part in forging the reputations of these acts, representing the 'Cream[x]' of the coolest music of the 1960s.

*

Moving back into the centre of town, the Marquee Club in Wardour Street Soho, where both the Stones and The Who (among many other British beat boom bands) played, is now a bar. The entrance to the next-door block of loft apartments is graced with a memorial plaque to incandescently wild Who drummer Keith Moon who died young battling alcoholism. Our chapter by Charlotte Banks documents the very first official "Rollin' Stones" gig at the original Marquee premises in Oxford Street in July 1962, a few months after Jagger and Richards first met Jones in Ealing. The Soho venue would later play a part in the metamorphosis of the 'New Yardbirds' into rock gods Led Zeppelin.

Just down Oxford Street from the first home of the Marquee is the 100 Club, one of the few key London venues which has retained its location for rock's 60 diamond years. Richard Luck chronicles the ups and downs of the 100 Club over those years – a legendary West End venue that has nurtured the development of Trad. jazz, British blues rock, prog rock, punk, and hair metal, among other genres. In 2010, Paul McCartney played a two-hour benefit set at the club when it became threatened with closure by pressure from high central

---

i. ix   http://news.bbc.co.uk/local/berkshire/hi/people_and_places/music/newsid_8438000/8438782.stm

i. x   Pun intended: Clack describes how Cream featuring Clapton, Bruce and Baker were also part of Ricky-Tick history.

INTRODUCTION

The Flamingo Club

London property taxes. The Club gained a reprieve, and in 2020, owner Jeff Horton was able to announce: "Westminster Council has made the 100 Club the first ever Grassroots Music Venue to be awarded Localism Relief. This award means that the venue will now be given 100% Business Rates relief for the entire time it remains at its current location at 100 Oxford Street, its home since 1942."

Another central London club which made a contribution to rock's formative years in the early 1960s was the Flamingo *(above)*, described by British blues legend John Mayall as "a very dark and evil-smelling basement... It had that seedy sort of atmosphere and there was a lot of pill-popping. You usually had to scrape a couple of people off the floor when you emerged into Soho at dawn..." The club resurfaced in contemporary culture as the venue for a fight between two of Christine Keeler's admirers, featured in the movie *Scandal*.

In 2013, promoter Pete Feenstra, together with John O'Leary & Alan Glen Allstars, recreated the glory R&B days of the Flamingo at the Bull's Head, Barnes, an extant West London suburban venue probably better known for its jazz heritage, but it also played an important part in the development of British blues-rock. In 2003, the pub was featured in the documentary episode *Red White & Blues* directed for Martin Scorsese's PBS series on the history of the blues by Mike Figgis. Scottish R&B boom singer Lulu sings Henry Glover's *Drown in my Own Tears* – a song made famous by Ray Charles and Aretha Franklin, among other artists – over a series of soundbites from great names in British blues – Eric Clapton, Mick Fleetwood, and John Mayall to name a few – all asserting the power that the British R&B invasion had to bring music of black origin to a wider US audience. Finally, one of the best-known US electric bluesmen, B B King himself, pops up to thank the British Invasion musicians for making him famous.

Poster for Back to the Flamingo

INTRODUCTION

A 2007 BBC documentary *How Britain Got the Blues* reflects a later change in editorial attitude. It features commentaries from Chris Barber, Yardbirds' Chris Dreja, and Manfred Mann's Tom McGuinness, among others, musing with a degree of self-effacing wokeness upon the apparent absurdity of young British kids emulating the music of African America. That absurdity is subsumed with a peculiarly British even-handedness: the central message being, as articulated by Phil May and Dick Taylor (The Pretty Things), that emerging British R&B musicians were interpreting the blues in a way that gratified suburban British (and later US) teens beyond prior measure.

Very few London venues can boast to have hosted live music almost every night since 1963. The Half Moon in Putney is one of those select few. Patrick Humphries takes us through the Half Moon's story from its beginnings as 'Folksville', a folk/blues club founded by artists Gerry Lockran, Royd Rivers, and Cliff Aungier. A gig at the Half Moon remains a badge of honour for aspiring UK musicians on the way up, or as a nostalgic nod to the past for old rockers.

West London nurtured notable female performers from the beat boom. The young Mary O'Brien (better known as 'blue-eyed soul' singer Dusty Springfield) is commemorated at the gates of Ealing Fields school with a plaque on the site of the convent school she attended in the late 1950s. O'Brien's fellow Hampstead native, Marianne Faithfull, who schooled in nearby Reading, began her commercial career managed by Stones' impresario Andrew Oldham, with the Jagger-Richards composition *As Tears Go By*.

Another singer who was given a break by Oldham and the Stones was Cleo Sylvestre. Italia-Conti-trained Sylvestre grew up in London, from three generations of showbusiness women. Sylvestre's mother danced regularly at the Shim-Sham Club, "London's miniature Harlem," later the site of the Flamingo Club, where Sylvestre met and was befriended by members of the Rolling Stones in 1963. In a 2021 interview[xi], Sylvestre relates how she was called by Mick Jagger to record at one of the Stones' early sessions with Decca in 1964. "In one take," she says, she cut a cover of Phil Spector's *To know Him is to Love Him*, backed by the 'Andrew Oldham Orchestra', aka Wyman, Jones, Watts, and Richards. "Oldham chose the song because he was a great admirer of Spector," she notes. In 2018, Sylvestre and her band Honey B Mama played Ealing Blues Festival, founded and curated by Ealing native musician Robert Hokum, who writes on his adolescence in the cradle of British R&B later in this book.

Manchester-born singer Elkie Brooks was 'discovered' by empresario Don Arden, and also began her recording career in London with Decca in 1964. Brooks guested and toured regularly with the Artwoods, and with Newcastle band the Animals, who had moved to London in 1964.

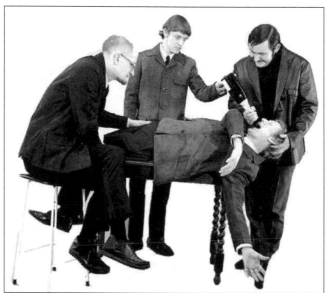

The Graham Bond Organisation *L-R* Dick Heckstall-Smith, Jack Bruce, Graham Bond, *(lying down)* Ginger Baker

---

> **KLOOKS KLEEK**
> **Railway Hotel, West Hampstead**
> **AMERICAN BLUES STAR**
> **BUDDY GUY**
> **ROD STEWART**
> **THE SOUL AGENTS**
> **plus THE BOBO LINKS**
> (Over 18s only). 6/-

The London Decca studios occupied premises at 165 Broadhurst Gardens NW6,[xii] adjacent to The Railway pub by West Hampstead station. From 1961-70 upstairs at the Railway was the home of 'Klooks Kleek', a jazz club named, phonetically, after beebop drummer Kenny Clarke's 1956 album.

From September 1963 the club began hosting funky, soulful, R&B in the particular shape of Georgie Fame & the Blue Flames and The Graham Bond Organisation, as well as other performers already mentioned in this introduction. Many live recordings of great rock music were made at KK; rumour has it that Decca installed a line direct from the club into their studios next door. The factual record contains some of the best-known live work by Bond, Mayall, Zoot Money, and Cream, to name a few, released on other labels or as bootlegs.

The Railway continued to build its musical reputation in the 70s and 80s as the host of the Starlight (upstairs) and Moonlight (downstairs) Clubs, notable for early appearances from Elvis Costello, U2, and Joy Division.

Jazz music continued fertile development in London clubs during rock's diamond decade, often crossing paths with its upstart nephew genre. Ronnie Scott's was founded in 1959 at 39 Gerrard St, Soho, moving to its larger present premises in Frith St in 1965. On 16th Sept 1970, two nights before his

i. xii   Now used by the English National Opera

untimely death, a restless Jimi Hendrix jammed at Scott's with his ex-Animals friend Eric Burdon's band War. War's guitarist Howard Scott (no relation) recalls: "[Jimi's] eyes were just so white and wide open. He was ready to play. We started jamming a song called 'Mother Earth,' it was this hardcore blues and Jimi lit into a guitar solo. Me and Jimi were just cutting the place up...[xiii]"

As well as international jazz greats including Nina Simone and Sarah Vaughan, Scott's has nurtured jazz-fusions in the persona of bands and artists such as Brand X, Ernest Ranglin, Monty Alexander, Dick Morrissey, and Jim Mullen. Chelsea's 606 Club also continues to offer the best in jazz, R&B, blues, and gospel, as does the PizzaExpress Jazz Club in Dean St, Soho, opened in 1968 by the restaurant company's founder Peter Boizot.

The contribution to the history of rock music made by the South-West-London-based musicians, who turned rhythm and blues into popular dance music for suburban teenagers in the early 1960s – and then exported their sound back to the USA – is indisputable. Without the transatlantic cross-fertilisation that took place in that decade, classic albums such as *Pet Sounds, Mr Tambourine Man, Sgt Pepper's Lonely Hearts Club Band, Let it Bleed,* Janis Joplin's *Cheap Thrills,* or Patti Smith's *Horses* would never have been made. Growing up with this music we had no idea what a truly privileged generation we were. In this book we celebrate the extraordinary contribution of those musicians and remember the many venues from the centre to the South and West of London that helped British R&B to flourish.

---

i. xiii   https://www.rollingstone.com/music/music-news/jimi-hendrix-final-performance-ronnie-scotts-documentary-1290409/

Inside the Half Moon, Putney
Photo: Edwardx

Blues Incorporated *Left to Right:* Cyril Davies, Charlie Watts, Alexis Korner, Andy Hoogenboom, Keith Scott, 1962

THE EALING CLUB

Alistair Young

"The Ealing Club and Blues Incorporated were heavy influences on just about everybody, but especially on Fleetwood Mac, Cream, the Yardbirds, Manfred Mann, John Mayall and the Pretty Things."

– Ronnie Wood

The opening on 17 March 1962 of the Ealing Blues Club by Alexis Korner and Cyril Davies is generally regarded as the pivotal moment when British 'electric blues' developed its own identity. Local youngsters who came to the club were given a rare opportunity to see a range of British artists playing American blues music for the first time.

These kids would go on to form bands that tried to emulate American blues guitar artists using amplified electric guitar, thumping bass, screaming vocals and pounding drums … and a bit of harmonica. The scene became known in London from 1962 onwards as the rhythm and blues scene thanks in part to Alexis Korner and Cyril Davies' admiration of the Black American blues artists whose music they so much admired.

The club became a testing ground for many of the musicians who would go on to become legendary in the world of music. Bands such as the Rolling Stones, Manfred Mann, and The Who cut their teeth here while other key participants would later contribute to supergroups such as Cream and the

Ginger Baker on drums, c. 1965

Jimi Hendrix Experience and go on to front highly influential bands such as The Animals.

From 1962-65 the basement venue, opposite Ealing Broadway Station, became synonymous with the R&B revival and is often mentioned by the leading lights of British music within keynote interviews and biographies.

Perhaps most significant is the meeting at the club of teenagers Mick Jagger and Keith Richards from Dartford in South London with musician Brian Jones from Cheltenham. They would start to jam together and go on to form a band. From April 1962 to the end of March '63, the venue became the meeting point, the jamming room, and blues hub for the musicians that would form the greatest rock 'n' roll band of all time –the Rolling Stones.

The success of the Ealing Club's R&B programme and Blues Incorporated soon spread to other live music 'Trad jazz' clubs such as the Marquee Club, the Flamingo & the Eel Pie

Island Hotel. It quickly inspired impresarios too, to set up venues such as the Crawdaddy and the Ricky-Tick to cater for the new R&B sound.

The Stones were early players, surrounded by so many others, who soon picked up the blues influences that would feed into the sound of classic rock in the 60s and 70s. In particular, it was the drummers associated with the Ealing Club who were true pioneers of the new R&B sound: Charlie Watts, Ginger Baker, Keith Moon and Mitch Mitchell were all closely connected. Although influenced by jazz, by the end of the 70s, their distinctive styles formed the key chapters of any rock drumming textbook.

The Ealing 'Jazz' Club's legacy is taught by musicologists in Kansas University while *Mojo* magazine writer Paul Trynka eloquently summed up the club with the following line: "From the Rolling Stones to Led Zeppelin, Ealing is the Cradle of British Rock Music."

Ken Colyer on trumpet

It is no coincidence that a few miles away from the club in Hanwell, a small music and drum shop known as J & T Marshall began supplying guitar amplifiers to local teenagers such as Pete Townshend and John Entwhistle. Marshall Amplification played a key part in enabling rock music to be played to bigger audiences in bigger venues and they flourished alongside the meteoric rise of many of their customers.

BACKGROUND TO THE CLUB PRE-1962

From 1955-57 American rock 'n' roll arrived on British shores through the likes of Bill Haley, Elvis Presley, Buddy Holly, Little Richard, Jerry Lee Lewis and many others, influencing British youth culture in several ways. It quickly generated a host of UK equivalents such as Tommy Steele and Cliff Richard and the Shadows.

Post-war Britain had witnessed a growing interest in American jazz brought to these shores by American GIs, from the so-called 'Trad jazz scene' whose leading lights were Ken Colyer, Humphrey Lyttleton and Chris Barber (amongst many others). They pursued the sounds of the original New Orleans 'Dixieland' jazz bands and helped encourage club nights in towns across the country.

This 'Trad. jazz scene' contrasted and was sometimes at odds with the modern jazz movement that followed the bebop of Charlie Parker, Dizzy Gillespie and John Coltrane, and was led by British exponents Ronnie Scott and Johnny Dankworth.

From 1949, West London based Ken Colyer's Crane River Jazz Band became passionate devotees in search of jazz music roots. Colyer's eagerness to learn about the sounds of New Orleans led him to join the merchant navy, jump ship and break US visa regulations. His journey included a brief US stint with the American clarinettist George Lewis and led to the exploration of 'jug bands and Skiffle', skills and knowledge he brought back to London and expressed through both the Crane

River Jazz Band and the Chris Barber band. It was here that both Alexis Korner and Lonnie Donegan would experiment with sets based on these skiffle roots with Lonnie Donegan going on to become the face of the UK skiffle movement, topping charts in the UK and US with Rock Island Line.

At its height of popularity the UK derivative of skiffle had moved well beyond the blues roots discovered by Colyer, taking on influences from country music and even English music hall tradition. As with many commercially successful music movements the purists such as Ken Colyer and Alexis Korner became disillusioned with the scene as they felt the original roots expressed by the likes of Leadbelly and many before had been left behind. Nevertheless, the UK skiffle craze got kids from across the UK into the idea of picking up and playing guitar in a DIY culture like no other before. Lennon and McCartney, Jimmy Page and Wilko Johnson and everyone else became enthralled with playing music.

Alexis Korner: Photo Heinrich Klaffs

ALEXIS KORNER & CYRIL DAVIES

Cyril Davies

From the early 1950s Alexis Korner cut his own 'musical teeth' within Ken Colyer's Jazzmen and the Chris Barber Jazz Band, where he stood in for the figurehead of 'Skiffle' Lonnie Donegan. Alexis himself helped pioneer skiffle participating in the first British Skiffle album in November 1954 as part of Ken Colyer's band. (Decca LP 1196)

Meanwhile, in September 1955, Cyril Davies had set up the London Skiffle Club above the Roundhouse pub in Soho where Alexis Korner would become a regular visitor.

By 1957, both had become disillusioned with the Skiffle movement and converted this venue to an acoustic blues club that would become known as the 'Blues and Barrelhouse Club'. It was here that illustrious visitors would include the likes of Big Bill Broonzy, Muddy Waters, Champion Jack Dupree and Country singer Ramblin' Jack Elliott, many of whom also became regular guests at Alexis Korner's Bayswater residence.

MUDDY WATERS AND CHRIS BARBER

In 1958, when Muddy Waters toured the UK with Otis Spann they set off a small explosion. Audiences, seeking the more traditional acoustic sound of 'Country Blues', were dismayed at Muddy Waters' use of the electric guitar. Not many were ready for the use of electric amplification, something that had already come and gone in and out of fashion in South Chicago.

Chris Barber's initiative to manage and promote such tours is sometimes overlooked but thanks to the part he played in introducing so many artists to the UK, Barber gained the title 'Grandaddy of British Blues'. The impact of Muddy Waters' tour offered an opportunity for Alexis Korner and Cyril Davies to start playing a blues interval at the Marquee Club in London during Chris Barber's set in late 1961.

Throughout the 50s, Alexis Korner and Cyril Davies had been absorbing the blues through their extensive record collections and contact with American blues and folk cognoscenti with whom they chatted and jammed at their Wardour Street venue.

Although the electric blues of Sister Rosetta Tharpe and Muddy Waters inspired Alexis Korner and Cyril Davies to emulate the sound for London audiences, they were soon given their marching orders from The London Blues & Barrelhouse Club at the Roundhouse pub in Wardour Street, by a landlord who complained about the noise emanating from the upstairs function room. They understood that amplification was a game changer but they needed to find another venue.

AMPLIFIED BLUES GUITAR & BLUES INCORPORATED

The use of amplified electric guitars forced Alexis Korner to search for a venue away from the Trad. jazz strongholds of central London and it is believed that the idea of a basement drinking club in Ealing came about thanks to a tip-off from Art Wood, one of the many vocalists associated with Blues Incorporated.

Thanks to its media connections, Ealing was already a fertile place for live music. The Chris Barber Band, Acker Bilk and Kenny Ball were features at Ealing Town Hall and perhaps most significantly American blues legends Sonny Terry & Brownie McGhee performed their only London gig in Ealing in October 1961.

In late 1961, Alexis Korner encountered bassist Andy Hoogenboom and future Blues Incorporated drummer Charlie Watts during a gig at the Troubadour.

Alexis and Cyril also needed to find a home for Blues Incorporated and in late 1961 they would book rehearsal space with Ealing Club leaseholder, Fery Asgari.

THE SEEDS OF AN R&B BOOM

The *Jazz News* edition of 3rd January 1962, contains a small piece titled 'Korner Goes R&B' announcing his intentions to put experiments tried out with Chris Barber and Acker Bilk during intervals at the Marquee Club into a permanent formation to be named Blues Incorporated. The piece ends: 'I am looking for a really good modern blues singer in the Muddy Waters, Otis Spann, Chuck Berry tradition'.

In the following months at Ealing, he was going to find them!

14th March: *Jazz News* Advertises:

17th March: Alexis Korner's Blues Incorporated at the Ealing Club.

Alexis Korner, Cyril Davies, Andy Hoogenboom, Art Wood, Charlie Watts, Keith Scott, and Long John Baldry are the original members of the band that managed to fill the damp cellar bar that was known as Ealing Jazz Club or more colloquially as the 'moist hoist'.

It was trumpeter and taxi driver Wally Marshall who first brought in music to the venue, by helping set up afternoon jazz sessions in the late 1950s. A young Iranian student, Fery Asgari then put forward ideas for evening gigs. He became leaseholder of the club in 1960 and made all the agreements with Alexis Korner to set up blues club nights. He would arrange bookings with subsequent bands that visited the club.

Paul Pond (Paul Jones), later lead singer of Manfred Mann, would be one of the young singers to attend the first night of Blues Incorporated at Ealing.

24th March: Brian Jones attends the Ealing Club to see Blues Incorporated.

31st March: Brian Jones sits in with Blues Incorporated.

7th April: Alexis Korner introduces Brian Jones as slide guitarist Elmo Lewis and he plays *Dust my Broom* in front of an impressed Mick Jagger and Keith Richards who are attending the club after hearing of it in *Jazz News*. Also attending gigs at this time was Dick Taylor (first bassist with the Rolling Stones and later guitarist with the Pretty Things).

Eric Burdon (future lead singer of the Animals) hitchhiked down from Newcastle to attend the club and sing alongside Jagger. Both Dick Taylor and Eric Burdon are interviewed in the movie *Suburban Steps To Rockland; The Story of the Ealing Club* directed by Giorgio Guernier.

The Who at the Ealing Club with Fery Asgari, Club Manager, 1965

11th April: Blues Incorporated played their first intermission set at the Marquee Club. Around this time, Charlie Watts willingly lets Ginger Baker take over as drummer of Blues Incorporated, partly in admiration, but also to concentrate on the day job.

Jack Bruce auditioned at the Ealing Club for Blues Incorporated too, as discussed in his interview for the movie *Suburban Steps To Rockland – The Story of the Ealing Club*. Bruce stated that "thanks to this opportunity, I had a career in music."

19th May: Article in *Disc* magazine announcing that Mick Jagger will sing with the band on Saturdays at Ealing and Thursdays at the Marquee.

June: Mick Jagger starts to jam with Brian Jones and Ian Stewart. Keith Richards started performing around this time as well. In 2015, on the release of his solo album *Cross Eyed Heart*, four temporary plaques appeared to commemorate venues associated with the guitarist. One appeared at the Ealing Club declaring Keith Richard's first gig: https://www.ealingclub. com/2015/10/keith-richards-influence/kr/

11th July: *Jazz News* states that Mick Jagger will play with his band the Rolling Stones at the Marquee.

12th July: The Rolling Stones' first official gig at the Marquee Club. Brian Jones names the band the Rollin' Stones 'off the cuff' while arranging the booking by phone with the Marquee.

12th July: Blues Incorporated perform on BBC Jazz Club.

July: The second ever Rolling Stones gig is held at the Ealing Club, beginning a Saturday night residency that would stretch over the next 7-8 months. Pete Townshend (a regular visitor) stated, when interviewed by Melvyn Bragg, that he witnessed the first of these Saturday night gigs. (This event was qualified in a subsequent interview by the University of West London *Your University* Magazine (Winter 2021) when asked about the Ealing Club:

"I never saw them play there but I did see the Rolling Stones at Ealing Broadway Station walking across the road to do a show there in early 1963. They had a residency and the shows were packed – it was really where the Stones began. The person I was with thought they looked ugly but I thought they were the most beautiful men I'd ever seen. Not a bad band as it turned out"

The first of at least twenty-two gigs that were played from July 1962 – March 1963. Eric Clapton stood in on a regular basis for Mick Jagger and sang in Rolling Stones intervals.

October: Musical differences caused Blues Incorporated to split. Cyril Davies formed the All Stars to pursue his love for the Chicago blues style with the sound of the harmonica front and centre. He employed musicians such as Carlo Little, Nicky Hopkins and respected guitarist Bernie Watson (Screaming Lord Sutch's band). Alexis Korner pursued the sound of brass with the likes of Graham Bond, Dick Heckstall-Smith and Art Themen.

December: The Rolling Stones played Tuesday nights. London endured thick smog and ice in one of the coldest winters on record. Wally Marshall, (bar manager) reportedly let the band sleep on the cold damp floor of the Ealing Club, on condition that they leave the bar alone. Wally left them locked in the bar so he could find the warmth of his stove at the nearby Ealing Broadway taxi shelter. Around this time the band heard of a new bass player.

5th January 1963 – Bill Wyman says of this day in Ray Colemans's biography *Stone Alone*:

"Two vital moves clinched my arrival in the Stones as a full timer, although I was not to give up my day job for another eight and a half months. First, I decided to integrate myself into their 'club' by growing my hair longer and combing it forwards. A LOUD CHEER FROM MICK, KEITH and BRIAN greeted my arrival at the ABC café, our meeting spot next door to the

Ealing Jazz Club, just before our gig there on 5 January. I immediately felt more at home in their company, now that they had generated a bit of warmth."

Tuesday 12th January: A foreword written by Charlie Watts in the official 50th anniversary book of the Rolling Stones stated Charlie had his first gig with the band at the Ealing Club on this day. Tweets from the band have regularly celebrated Charlie's integration into the band on or around the 12th January. Charlie Watts was the last member to join up with Mick Jagger, Keith Richards, Brian Jones and Bill Wyman. Pianist Ian Stewart was also still in the line-up at this time.

Tuesday 15th January: Rolling Stones played the Ealing Club. In Keith Richard's biography *Life* he discusses the early formation of the Stones and states, "this day is the first mention of Charlie playing with us."

March 2nd: The last recorded Rolling Stones gig at the Ealing club. Following one formative year at the Ealing Club, the band moved on to the Crawdaddy Club at the Station Hotel, Richmond. Here, many have reported, they met numerous musicians, including John Lennon and Paul McCartney who

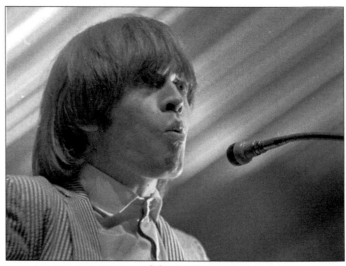

Brian Jones

would pen them a song… 'I Wanna Be Your Man'.

March: The Mann Hugg Blues brothers (later to become Manfred Mann) played their first gigs at the Ealing Club, beginning a nine-month residency. During this period they recorded two songs: *Why Should We Not?* and *Cock-a-Hoop*. They failed to chart.

January 1964: Manfred Mann's record '5-4-3-2-1' was adopted as the theme tune for *Ready Steady Go!* The song became a big hit and the band moved beyond Ealing. They became the first band from Southern England to form part of the British invasion of the USA.

The band did a return gig on June 4th 1964 just before their U.S. tour. Their new Hammond organ with Leslie speakers proved to be a logistical nightmare to fit into the small space.

By the end of 1962, the club had overseen the creation of the Rolling Stones who were brought together by Alexis Korner and played there over twenty times. Eric Clapton, and Pete Townshend played Ealing, as did many other members of future bands that would later take the rawer sound of rock to the world.

The Ealing Club played its part in the invention of that very sound with the first live performance ever to use the classic 'loud' Marshall JTM45 guitar amplifier one Sunday night in 1963. The band assembled to test the pre-production amp included future Jimi Hendrix Experience drummer Mitch Mitchell, who worked in the Marshall shop in Hanwell, and saxophonist Terry Marshall, the 'T' in 'JTM'.

The Ealing Club and Blues Incorporated led directly to the early 1960s British rhythm and blues boom, which created the more intense sounds that were to influence so many. This included the Beatles, who had already opened the gates in the US for the next wave of British bands. Groups such as the Rolling Stones, Cream, The Who, Manfred Mann, The Yardbirds, John Mayall, The Pretty Things, Fleetwood

Mac, The Animals and Free, all participated or were heavily influenced by the scene generated by the Ealing Club. In 1973, David Bowie indicated he had been on the scene in those early days (see write up on Pin Ups)

British R&B soon spread to other London venues, notably the Crawdaddy, Eel Pie Island, the Flamingo and the Marquee. In Ealing, the foundations for this movement were already established. Ealing resident Pete Townshend developed feedback on his guitars at the first Who gigs at the Oldfield Hotel (Greenford). He practised his auto-destructive art on the Marshall speakers sourced locally in the first Marshall shop in Hanwell.

His inspiration for destruction of guitars and amplifiers came from art classes attended at Ealing Art School (now the University of West London), where subsequent students would also include Ronnie Wood's brother Art Wood and Freddie Mercury. Gigs at this particular venue were a regular occurrence. In April 1969, there was a performance by David Bowie at the beginning of the most successful phase of his career. Later that year in the same UWL (University of West London) building Freddie Mercury made one of his first appearances as the frontman of a band. As a showman and musician Jimi Hendrix would be deeply influenced by the music of The Who and their contemporaries, even deciding to purchase his amplifiers from the Marshall shop in Hanwell.

Perhaps the following quote from the Keith Richards biography *Life* from 2010 says it all:

> "Cyril Davies and Alexis Korner got a club going, the weekly spot at the Ealing Jazz Club, where Rhythm and Blues freaks could conglomerate. Without them there might have been nothing."

Ealing has now been recognised as the place where 'blues rock' began. As Bill Wyman stated in his book, Blues Incorporated represented a new 'attitude'. The heavier rhythms and a rise in volume all took place in front of a young, impressionable Ealing Club crowd that included figures who would become the most influential rock musicians ever to leave British shores. Jagger, Richards, Jones, Clapton, Baker, Bruce, Townshend, Beck, to name a few. John Mayall gave up his day job, moved to London and surrounded himself with musicians who had already experienced the buzz of London's R&B scene. The tiny Ealing Club played host to John Mayall and The Bluesbreakers in their earliest days.

Alexis Korner's electric guitar, together with his band Blues Incorporated, helped to create the movement that would lead to a revival of American blues music. The 'British Invasion' by young white musicians to the US helped bring recognition in America and beyond for the so-called 'negro folk blues guitarists' who had for long been overlooked by mainstream America.

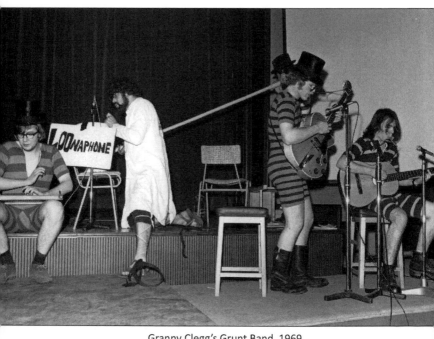

Granny Clegg's Grunt Band, 1969
Left to right: Charlie Couchman, Martin Stone, JEM Martin, Robert Hokum.
At the back Mike Cowley
Photo: Robert Hokum

AN ADOLESCENCE IN MUSIC

Robert Hokum

"The British feel of blues has been hard, rather than emotional. Far too much emphasis on 12 bar, too little attention to words, far too little originality."

– Alexis Korner

On March 13 1972 I got a gig with my college bandmates at Tabby's, which was the then name for the former premises of The Ealing Club. So almost exactly ten years after the founding of the Ealing Blues Club on 17 March 1962, I got to play on the spot where Alexis Korner and Cyril Davies had started the movement that was to be the dominating force on my life over that decade.

Although we knew of the history and that we were performing where famous people had started, doing the gig at Tabby's in 1972 didn't give me the sense of gravitas and heritage that it would when we started gigging there in 2011 to raise funds for 2012's 50th Anniversary Heritage Plaque. In '72 rock music was still in the ascendant, pub rock was developing, punk wasn't a music form and vinyl album sales were booming – just look at a list of the albums released in that year. You didn't really think about heritage when so much new music was happening. However, I was to cross paths with several musicians connected with the Ealing Club's legacy over the coming years.

By the time I left college in Summer '74, I'd found my 'niche' and had developed the skills that would eventually allow me to found the Ealing Blues Festival. This, in turn, would lead to my involvement in campaigning for the heritage plaques for The Ealing Club and Marshall Amps, as well as taking part in the documentary films *Suburban Steps To Rockland* and *Rock 'n' Roll Island – Where Legends Were Born* and, of course, in the 'Rock's Diamond Year' initiative.

What follows is a much-edited account of my musical life from 1962 to rock's 'Tin Anniversary Year' of 1972...

I was born in July 1951 in Ealing's Perivale Maternity Hospital.[xv] My parents had a one-bedroom flat in Elthorne Avenue, Hanwell, and the son of the family downstairs was a bit older than me and would later join a biker gang and be known as 'Evil Eric'. Thankfully, he probably forgot that when I was about three I hit him over the head with a small spade. But it got back to me that he once jokingly said, "I'm gonna get that Bob, he nicked one of my Dinky toys."

With the impending birth of a brother in 1956 the family moved to Coldershaw Road, West Ealing. I attended Oaklands School and had, I guess, a pretty normal 'upper working class' upbringing. Going to Cub Scouts, putting up with school bullies, scraped knees, family camping holidays... I don't recall being particularly interested in music at the time, but can remember Workers Playtime on the radio and Clinton Ford singing 'Fanlight Fanny'. Interestingly though, in the year below me at school was a gobby kid by the name of Lee John Collinson; Lee's family would subsequently move to Canvey Island and he would become Lee Brilleaux and form Dr. Feelgood.

In 1962, things changed. I'd become a School House Captain at Oaklands and one of only three kids there to get into Ealing County Grammar School, the top-rated school

i. xv   long since demolished, but at the time almost every other person one met entered the world there! (Kate Middleton's Mum was born there!)

in the Borough. For my 11th birthday the family finally got a record player. It was a Bush in the style of the classic Dansette. My first records were 'Wonderful Land' by The Shadows and 'Nut Rocker' by B. Bumble and The Stingers. For the first time I could listen to what I wanted to, as many times as I wanted to, and music started to mean something to me. By Christmas 1962, The Beatles were in the lower reaches of the charts, and the kids at school were talking about their older siblings going to see bands in some basement in Ealing Broadway (better known as The Ealing Club). Thus, as I became a music fan and record buyer, just down the road in one direction Alexis Korner and Cyril Davies were curating a musical revolution, while down the road in the other direction the Marshall music shop was embarking on a project that would redefine the electric guitar.

By 1963 the Stones had hit the charts with 'Come On' and *Ready Steady Go!* a popular music programme aimed at teenagers, had started on the TV. At the same time, I'd begun to see my own identity through this new emerging music

The Rolling Stones perform on *Ready Steady Go!* November 22, 1963

The Small Faces, 1966

scene. A year later my family moved to Southdown Avenue in Hanwell, and by then I was getting more and more into music. The local scene was becoming well established, with regular gigs being held at The Blue Triangle[xvi], The Feathers and of course the Ealing Club. As well as R&B, there was a thriving jazz scene and an emerging folk scene in the area. Kids at school were buying guitars, fuelling what became a substantial 'youth club' circuit. All my pocket money went on records, mainly by Manfred Mann or The Animals, who were my two favourite bands. Manfred Mann first played the Ealing Club in 1963, taking over a residency from the Rolling Stones who had moved on to The Crawdaddy in Richmond. But I was still too young to actually go to gigs…

By 1965 the bands playing the music that I liked were Mods! At one point I even styled myself on Steve Marriott from the Small Faces: checked pattern hipster trousers, and a centre parting (!) Thankfully, I don't think any photos exist.

i. xvi   A small club opposite Ealing Town Hall, where Ealing Filmworks now stands

Soul music from the States was also gaining in popularity, with Tamla Motown artists appearing in the charts. I was desperate to get to see live music. My friend from 'next-door-but-one' was a year older than me, he got to see the Rolling Stones at Greenford Granada (now Tesco). I wanted to go with him but my mother wouldn't have it. Manfred Mann played Hanwell Community Centre, I nagged and nagged Mum to let me go, she eventually agreed on condition that she went with me: "go to a gig with one's mum?!" I would never have lived it down at school! I didn't go; Mum would have been all of 37 at the time…1966 was another defining year. I'd changed Scout Groups to Hanwell Methodist Venture Scouts who were mainly older than me. A couple of them had motor bikes and, of course, rocker-style leather jackets. That was the point at which my 'mod' gear went, although I still preferred soul music to the rock 'n' roll that they were more into! Having said that, they were a great bunch of blokes, although they could be rather 'rough and rowdy'. Mum didn't like them, but I have some fond memories of our misbehaviour.

On my 15th birthday I'd scraped enough money together to buy a guitar. A cheap nylon-string affair from Squires Music of Ealing. I should have bought a steel-string model, but I had no-one to advise me and my parents weren't interested. I was failing academically, despite having been one of the brightest at primary school. Ealing County Grammar School for Boys was a hideous place, I had few friends there; many of the pupils were from wealthier families and a snobbish culture existed. I far preferred the company of my working-class mates at Scouts. Against this background, although my love of music grew, my musical ability was negligible and didn't progress.

But, in October '66, I became eligible for a National Insurance number. I got it and one phone call later had a Saturday job at Bentalls department store in Ealing Broadway (Dusty Springfield had also had a Saturday job there). Economic freedom! I could now go to gigs and pay for them myself. Being into Soul music, my crowd were fans of Ike & Tina Turner who had just had a hit with 'River Deep, Mountain High'. They were playing The Albert Hall with some other bands who we weren't that bothered about, but we had to go. This was my first live gig, and here's the line-up. First on – Peter Jay & The Jaywalkers with Terry Reid on vocals, second act – the full Ike and Tina Turner Revue with The Ikettes, third act – The Yardbirds with Jimmy Page and Jeff Beck, closing act – the Rolling Stones.

The Ike & Tina Turner Revue were fantastic, the Rolling Stones were inaudible because of the screaming fans (there's film of this and we were in row 12, down the front!), but this was the night I became a Jeff Beck fan, and here's why. 1966 was when the bands who had previously dressed in a 'mod' style were now sporting more 'hippy' dress: Keith Relf was wearing a purple velvet jacket, Jimmy Page a white trouser suit. Beck was the last member to appear and out of the wings he came, unshaven and wearing a scruffy Yardbirds t-shirt, with a scowl he plugged a Les Paul into a Marshall stack, touched the guitar headstock against the speaker cabinet and turned it up until feedback, then turned round to face the audience and hit the riff from 'Over Under Sideways Down'. The 15-year-old

Ike and Tina Turner, Hamburg 1972 Photo: Heinrich Klaffs

me thought that he was just so cool!

Soon after this initiation into 'live' music I was regularly going to gigs at youth club dances. The band that could fill any church hall in Ealing was The Fulson Stilwell Blues Band: a blues band with a brass section playing church hall youth clubs! You don't get that these days! This would have been the first time that I heard a band play tunes by artists like Freddie King. Although only a few years older, they were regarded as local heroes by my group of friends. They split in 1969, but they have a Facebook page with plenty of 60s pictures on it.

The youth clubs of that period were where those of us at single-sex schools went to meet girls. But, of course, we were naïve and usually failed miserably. With 16 being the age at which one could ride a scooter, there were frequently gangs of Mods in attendance, although by 1967 this was a declining trend with many gravitating towards skinhead culture. This involved a lot of aggressive posturing. Frequently at school there would be talk along the lines of how "the Wembley Boys done the Greenford Boys up at the Starlite Ballroom."

As for me, I was still into soul music but gravitating towards the emerging hippy culture (although long hair wasn't allowed at Ealing Grammar), and my best mates were rockers.

Opposite the premises of The Ealing Club was The Feathers pub, now a MetroBank (in '67 The Pink Floyd played there). I never went to any of the gigs but was certainly familiar with its cellar bar, which was a hotbed of under-age drinking (and everything that went with it) for hordes of schoolkids who could say that they were 18 and keep a straight face. Underage drinking was rife: I ordered my first pint over a bar at age 15 in The Grange on Ealing Common.

Music lessons at Ealing Grammar were pretty grim and of no relevance to my musical tastes. I did actually drop out of music in favour of engineering drawing but was still trying to teach myself guitar. A nylon-string guitar was not the best instrument to learn on: trying to do fingerstyle incorporations of Steve Cropper/Duck Dunn parts was beyond my abilities. There were plenty of kids at Ealing Grammar with rich parents who had bought them really good guitars. One pupil in the same year as me, Pete Wakefield, (a nice bloke, a rarity at Ealing Grammar) had a Fender Guitar and a Gibson amp. On weekends, he'd play in the house band at The Top Rank in Watford with a keyboard player by the name of Rick Wakeman who was a pupil at another local grammar school, Drayton Manor, in Hanwell.

I managed to scrape together enough 'O' Level exam passes to get into the 6th form but my last two years at Ealing Grammar ('67-'69) were marked by a further academic decline. However, thanks to the money from the Saturday job, I went to some amazing gigs in that time. The Stax revue with Otis Redding, Sam & Dave, Booker T. and others at Hammersmith Odeon, Aretha Franklin at Hammersmith Odeon, Hendrix at The Saville Theatre on the night Brian Epstein died, Led Zeppelin at Farx in the back room of The Northcote Arms, Southall and countless more at venues like Eel Pie Island Hotel and the Marquee. I also remember seeing The Bonzo Dog Band at Acton Town Hall and Quintessence at Ealing Town Hall.

Another band with local connections was Fleetwood Mac – John McVie having attended Walpole Grammar School in West Ealing. One of his cousins went to Ealing Grammar and he showed me the 12-bar blues. My guitar playing remained dreadful, but I did join the school tiddlywinks team, only making it as a reserve. As I recall, they were beaten in the National Finals by Bradford Girls Grammar: thankfully I didn't have to share that shame... But I smashed it at the Hanwell Methodist Youth Club Tiddlywinks Championship!

In July 1969, I left Ealing Grammar with 'A' level passes in Maths and Engineering Drawing. The careers officer was hopeless and just asked me what my dad did for a living. Also, my parents had informed me that they weren't going to support me at college. So reluctantly, I accepted an engineering apprenticeship with Humphreys & Glasgow Petrochemicals which involved enrolling on an HND Course in Engineering at Twickenham College of Technology (aka 'Twick Tech'). I was never cut out for engineering, as anyone who has ever witnessed me attempting to do DIY will testify, and little did I know then that Twick Tech may have been one of the best things that could have happened to me.

Back in those days, students were given an afternoon every week of 'liberal studies' activities. The college principal at Twick Tech was a music lover and had appointed a Scotsman, Cameron McNicol, as Head of Music Liberal Studies. Cameron had come from a working-class background, and was a talented classical musician but he understood that as long as people loved music it really didn't matter what they played or how well they played it. He had equipped out the music facility with listening booths, Fender guitar amps and employed some part-time music teachers, in particular bassist Martin Lowenthal

Fleetwood Mac, 1968

and trumpeter Fred Jamieson. Over the next couple of years, Cameron, Martin and Fred would show me music theory, stagecraft, and even took me out on gigs. They mentored me, and to them I owe an immeasurable debt of gratitude.

By 1969, the Twickenham/Richmond area had taken over from Ealing as the music counterculture centre – the Eel Pie Island Club in particular being *the* place to go. I went to many gigs at the Eel Pie Island Hotel and saw the likes of Black Sabbath and Deep Purple there. Twickenham Film Studios had been used by The Beatles to make two of their films and while they were in the area they had gone to Richmond's Crawdaddy Club to see the Rolling Stones perform. There were thriving folk and jazz scenes in the area and Twick Tech was right on top of this, spawning some excellent acts across all genres, supported by the aforementioned Music Liberal Studies team.

Arriving at Twick Tech in Autumn '69 I immediately fell in with a 'bad crowd' of classmates, and we soon formed my first band, an anarchic jug/skiffle outfit entitled Granny Clegg's Grunt Band. We wore Edwardian bathing costumes and played a variety of instruments: from washboards to a toilet bowl rigged up with a trumpet mouthpiece as a kind of alpine horn/jug (you had to be there….). Our college gigs were alcohol-fuelled mayhem, but great fun. One of the first gigs we played outside of college was The Booze Drop at the White Hart in Acton, run by Rick Wakeman.

By Summer '71 I was playing with various folk acts, played with the college jazz musicians, got an electric guitar and formed a 'joke' rock 'n' roll band 'Rock Salmons and The Chips'! There were plenty of gigs to go to at the local colleges, St Marys, Maria Grey, Kingston Poly etc. as well as Twick Tech.

Then, the inevitable happened, I got slung out of Twick Tech for not going to lectures. My employers transferred me to a lower HNC course at Wandsworth Technical College (not a patch on Twick Tech!). A lifestyle of going to gigs and playing the guitar had caught up with me. I was still 19, at an age when one often has a sense of invulnerability and predestiny until getting a reality check, which was exactly what I had.

Autumn '71 to Summer '72 was really the first time that I realised that I had to 'shit or get off the pot' and over that period I re-took and passed the physics 'A' level that I'd failed at school, got 'A' level Economics at evening class, and passed the HNC in Mechanical Engineering. I then quit the apprenticeship and took an admin job for the import division of Komatsu Tractors.

Despite my newfound academic discipline, I did find time to be inspired by performances by John Martyn, Arthur Brown, Captain Beefheart, Screaming Lord Sutch, Focus and more. On August 5th 1972 I was a steward at The London Rock 'n' Roll Festival in Wembley so I saw Chuck Berry, Little Richard, Jerry Lee Lewis, Bill Haley, Bo Diddley – and got paid for it.

I was still seeing my bandmates at Twick Tech and on March 13 '72 we played that gig at Tabby's, the former premises of The Ealing Club. Having been a paid apprentice for three years with my parents not contributing to my upkeep meant that I'd become eligible for a 'mature student's grant'. So, what did I do? Simple, with my now four 'A' levels, I enrolled on an HND

Chuck Berry, London, 1972

Business Studies course at, you guessed it – Twickenham Tech. I think the Liberal Studies Music Department was glad to see me back!

In my first year of Business Studies, subjects included the law of contract and accountancy. I was very good at both. Then in '73 I was voted in as Social Secretary of the students' union, promoting and running the entertainments, a post which required negotiation, budgeting, marketing, stage management – the whole range of business disciplines. With the help and moral support of Cameron McNicol, who was still Head of Liberal Studies Music, I made a success of it. The only act I lost money on was Bert Jansch but for my Rag Ball in '74 had a 'sell out' for the Tremeloes who'd had over ten top-twenty hits.

As for my guitar playing, I was now good enough to have backed an opera singer at the Festival of Richmond and be in a band doing Django Reinhardt's style of music. Even after leaving college and getting 'jobs in the city', connections to the Ealing / Eel Pie scene would still keep appearing in my life.

In the mid-70s I regularly went to the Thursday sessions at the White Bear in Hounslow. These were run by Don Craine, founder of the Downliners Sect, Eel Pie Island and Ealing Club veterans and quoted as influences by David Bowie and Van Morrison. This was where I started doing solo gigs and further developing stagecraft. Don and I stayed in touch over the years and of course jammed when we started gigs at the Ealing Club premises in 2011.

In 1977, I was working for International Talent Booking as an agent, handling the gigs for The Tom Robinson Band (TRB) who would have major chart success with the catchy '2-4-6-8 Motorway'. What I didn't know then, was that Tom took up music as a direct result of meeting Alexis Korner. After TRB split in '79 I had no contact with Tom until he turned up at The Ealing Club plaque unveiling on 17 March 2012.

During my time at the talent agency from '76 to '79 I would look after some of the acts handled by Bill Curbishley who managed The Who. This lead to my meeting Peter Meaden, who managed them in the Ealing Club days and to spending an evening with Keith Moon in the Red Lion pub in Mayfair.

The 1980s came and I left the music industry for a variety of reasons and ended up in Fleet Street. I'd thought that the music industry of the 70s was bonkers, but it was minor league compared to the expense account bacchanalia of pre-Wapping Fleet Street. I was an advertising sales rep and at the next desk was a rep who played saxophone and had gigged with some great players. He joined my band.

One of the regular gigs that we got was at The Granville (now a Sainsburys) on Ealing Common, we did alternate Wednesdays with a band fronted by Simon Townshend, brother of Pete!

Monday 12 Dec 1988: got a gig at 'The Rock Over London' Xmas Party at The Crown & Sceptre in W1 and on that night had the pleasure of jamming with Jack Bruce!

Through my Fleet Street job, I dealt with a lot of advertising agencies and got several party gigs. On November 13 1990 we did a charity gig for Boase Massimi Pollitt agency at The Dover Street Wine Bar in Mayfair. Also appearing were Manfred Mann musos Paul Jones and Tom McGuinness, and a particular highlight was backing them both. These were the guys that took over from the Stones at The Ealing Club, the band that my Mum wouldn't let me see at Hanwell Community Centre and the first album that I ever bought was *The Five Faces of Manfred Mann.*

In 1996 I started DJ'ing at blues weekends at Warners Holiday Camps (*Hi De Hi....*) One of the regulars was pianist Ben Waters who I've subsequently gigged with on many occasions! In 2011 he released 'Boogie 4 Stu', a tribute to Stones keyboard player Ian Stewart with contributions from

Robert Hokum, The Cabbage Patch Pub, Twickenham, 1974.

Mick, Keith, Charlie, Ron & Bill…. We've done a few gigs together at the old Ealing Club premises to riotous fans from Belgium, Argentina and Brazil. Obviously when Ben gigs with members of the Stones, the guitar spot is filled, but he did get me to play rhythm guitar for the Ben Waters Big Band featuring ex-Stone Mick Taylor at The Henley Festival in July 2016.

Through the involvement with the campaign to install The Ealing Club plaque and the film *Suburban Steps to Rockland*, I got to say 'hello' to Charlie Watts (headline drummer at the first gig I ever went to!) and have made many acquaintances with people from that 'golden era'. Most notably Terry Marshall (of Marshall Amps fame) who was there at the beginning – I even did MC duties at Terry's 75th birthday bash.

AN ADOLESCENCE IN MUSIC

I started what was to become The Ealing Blues Festival in 1987. Over the years it became the successor to the legacy of The Ealing Blues Club and I was able to give gigs to many of the artists who had been part of the movement that it kicked off, e.g. Carlo Little (Screaming Lord Sutch's drummer who turned down the Stones), The Animals, Zoot Money, The Nashville Teens, Ali McKenzie (singer with Ronnie Wood's band The Birds), Manfred Mann's Paul Jones, The Downliners Sect and many more, playing alongside the younger bands who would take the music to the next generation.

Now in 2022, living in Twickenham, not far from Eel Pie Island, I wonder how my daughters (aged 24 and 20 at the time of writing) will look back on their adolescence. I was certainly defined by my 'adolescence in music' which has me still gigging at the age of 70 and has taken me to appear in such diverse places as Brixton Prison, Brecon Cathedral and the House of Commons, but the anecdotes about those are for another time.

The Guv'nors at the 2008 Ealing Blues Festival
Left-right: Sam Adams, Graham Wright, Robert Hokum, Tim Penn
Photo: John Sturrock

The Eel Pie Island Hotel c. 1960

THE EEL PIE ISLAND HOTEL
& THE EEL PIE CLUB

Gina Way

"I'll never forget the feeling as you got about halfway over the bridge, and you'd suddenly realise you were in the middle of a swelling crowd of people who all looked vaguely the same. There was a tremendous sense of belonging back then."

– Eric Clapton

"Hey, Mum, I'm going over to Jane's to do homework." Half an hour later, I am on the 33 bus from Sheen to Twickenham where I make my way to The Prince's Head (called The Barmy Arms by the locals) on Twickenham's Riverside, the meeting place for all the cool arty types before they embark on the walk over the footbridge to Eel Pie Island. It is 1963, and I am 16 years old.

The Island already had a reputation as the place to keep your teenage daughters away from at all costs, plus there had recently been an exposé in the *Evening Standard* of the long-haired types who smoked weed and impregnated young ladies at the Eel Pie Island Jazz Club so, naturally, The Island was off-limits as far as our parents were concerned!

We arrive at the far end of the footbridge. "Evening dear." "Thank you dear." say the two little old ladies with multiple

The footbridge across from Twickenham to Eel Pie Island

layers of clothes on, as we paid our one penny bridge toll.

Five minutes' walk along the Eel Pie Island path and we reach the Eel Pie Island Hotel, standing in all its faded glory on the other side of the Island, facing Ham across the river.

Arthur Chisnall, the owner of the Club, stands inside the entrance with one of his assistants. I fumble around in my handbag trying to get together the 1s/6d entrance fee. I am embarrassed. "I only have 11 pence halfpenny." "Oh! (sigh). Come in," says Arthur.

We have a peek in the main bar with its black footprints on its cream ceiling and say hello to some of the blokes we know from L'Auberge (the trendy coffee bar in Richmond) who are downing their pints of Newcastle Brown. We then descend some steps into the dance hall, with its rough plaster and cream paint, with arches down the left hand side. Straight ahead is the stage with the multi-coloured mural behind it. Above the stage is a plaster wall with a little window, which serves as the band's dressing room. Adjacent to the stage is the cloakroom and round the corner, on the right is the dance hall bar.

Playing tonight is Long John Baldry and the Hoochie Coochie Men, featuring Rod the Mod aka Rod Stewart on vocals. Rod is still mingling with his friends, and Long John Baldry calls him to the stage – "Come on, Phyllis," he bellows. How we love the music! As we dance the 'Island Stomp', the wooden floor bounces in time with the beat. In the interval we sit outside on the grass by the river, smoke whatever is to hand and chat to friends. How lucky we are! I am home by 11 o clock.

The Eel Pie Island Hotel had been a tourist attraction in the 19th century and, renowned for its sprung ballroom floor, was hosting tea dances during the 1920s and 1930s. However, by the mid-1950s it had fallen into disrepair and its owner, Michael Snapper, was not sure what to do with it. It was The Grove Jazz Band, led by trumpet player, Brian Rutland, who first had the idea of starting a jazz club on The Island in 1956. This was an accolade gradually bestowed on Arthur Chisnall, a Kingston junk-shop-owner who became involved

Inside The Eel Pie Island Hotel dance hall

The Rolling Stones perform at The Eel Pie Island Hotel

in organising weekly dances there a few months later. But it was Arthur who brought fame to the Club as a result of his social work in giving young people a voice and encouraging them to seek further education, sometimes against all odds. A jazz fan himself, he brought in name acts like Ken Colyer, Kenny Ball, Acker Bilk and George Melly.

In 1961, Alexis Korner and Cyril Davies founded the first home-grown rhythm and blues outfit, Blues Incorporated, at The Ealing Club, across the road from Ealing Broadway Station from whence started the British rhythm and blues boom. By 1962, Arthur Chisnall (contrary to his own taste in music) was persuaded to put on R&B bands on The Island on Wednesdays and Sundays, whilst the jazz bands continued to play on Saturdays. From 1962 to 1967, major names in British rhythm and blues appeared on The Island – such as Cyril Davies.

Rhythm & Blues All Stars, Long John Baldry's Hoochie Coochie Men (with Rod Stewart), the Rolling Stones, John Mayall's Bluesbreakers (featuring Eric Clapton), David Bowie (then known as David Jones), the Downliners Sect, and the Tridents (featuring Jeff Beck).

In 1967, The Eel Pie Island Jazz Club was forced to close because Arthur Chisnall could not meet the £200,000 worth of repairs which the Council had deemed necessary to make it safe, and squatters soon moved in to the Hotel. Two years later, in 1969, the Club was reopened briefly by Caldwell Smythe under the name of Colonel Barefoot's Rock Garden, welcoming progressive bands like Black Sabbath, Atomic Rooster, Deep Purple, Mott The Hoople, and the Edgar Broughton Band. But, by this time, a hippy commune of around a hundred squatters had congregated on the site and the hotel fell into rapid decay.

In 1971, following a demolition order by the Council, the Eel Pie Island Hotel burnt down 'in mysterious circumstances'. Nobody knows whether or not it was an accident, but one thing is for sure – it wasn't for the insurance – as no company would have insured it!

Squatters at the Eel Pie Island Hotel c. 1970

The Cabbage Patch Pub, Twickenham, now home to The Eel Pie Club

THE EEL PIE CLUB

Fast forward 27 years to 1998. The Museum of Richmond is curating an exhibition commemorating 35 years since the Rolling Stones played at The Station Hotel in Richmond and Eel Pie Island in Twickenham. Having been promoting dance and musical theatre extravaganzas for charity with my partner, Warren Walters, for the previous ten years, and overflowing with nostalgia for my teenage memories of seeing the Rolling Stones on The Island, I persuade Warren that we should put on a concert featuring a famous 60s rhythm and blues band with profits to benefit the museum. The museum gave us the contact of bass player and 60s music aficionado, Peter Moody, who in turn put us in contact with The Yardbirds, The Downliners Sect and Art Wood. And so begins our adventure…

We produced the first rhythm and blues concert since the 1960s at York House, Twickenham in July 1998. It was called 'From Rock 'n' Roll to Rhythm 'n' Blues' and featured The Bruvvers, The Downliners Sect with special guest, Art Wood, with The Yardbirds as the star act. The room capacity was four hundred people standing and we could have filled the room three times over. Many dignitaries from the R&B world were in attendance, including Giorgio Gomelsky (the Rolling Stones' and Yardbirds' original manager), Arthur Chisnall, owner of the Eel Pie Island Jazz Club, Harold and Barbara Pendleton, organisers of the Richmond Jazz Festival, and inventor Trevor Baylis.

Following a second sell-out concert at York House, this time featuring Stan Webb's Chicken Shack, we were approached by local slide guitarist/vocalist, Tom Nolan, who had played with his band, The Bluescasters, during the interval at both of our concerts. It was Tom's idea to start a rhythm and blues club that preserved the heritage of the music that started on Eel Pie Island. (I just take credit for naming it The Eel Pie Club!)

So, the Eel Pie Club was founded in April 2000. On the eve of the opening, Steve Hackett of Genesis turned up at our front door asking if he could jam with the band! (Er yes!) The Club's first home was The Room Above The Fox in Church Street, Twickenham. The Club quickly outgrew the space there and two months later we moved to its current premises at The Patch, above the Cabbage Patch pub on London Road, Twickenham. In 2009, the Eel Pie Club received the accolade of being voted 'Best Place to Hear Blues in England' by the Saturday *Guardian*.

In that same year, the Mayor of Richmond, Cllr Helen Lee-Parsons, in association with Richmond Council and The Eel Pie Club, erected a permanent heritage plaque on Twickenham Embankment, dedicated to the bands and musicians who played on Eel Pie Island, and the part played by Arthur Chisnall. The heritage plaque can be found adjacent to The Barmy Arms Public House, opposite Eel Pie Island. Eighteen Mayors and many musicians, including rock band Hawkwind, attended the unveiling of the site, which was followed by The Yardbirds performing a concert at the newly opened Live Room at Twickenham Stadium.

The following year, Tom Nolan moved away from the area and since then I have been running the Eel Pie Club with the assistance of Warren Walters. It is now in its 22nd year and has featured too many famous bands and musicians to mention, many of whom played on Eel Pie Island in its heyday. Bands have spanned the spectrum of rhythm and blues, blues and rock. Mentioning some of them would mean omitting others and all are equally important. The lifespan of the Eel Pie Island Jazz Club and Colonel Barefoot's Rock Garden combined, does not come close to the longevity of The Eel Pie Club.

In 2013, The Eel Pie Club was privileged to be invited by the Aurora Metro Charity to be assistant curator of their Lottery-funded Eelpiland Project which involved us in a

EEL PIE ISLAND HOTEL

The Eel Pie All-Stars, 2009

multitude of events such as appearing in the documentary *Rock 'n' Roll Island; Where Legends Were Born*, and writing a chapter in the book *The British Beat Explosion*, putting on special gigs featuring young bands at the Eel Pie Club, conducting walking tours of places of musical interest in Twickenham (with the assistance of storyteller extraordinaire, Don Craine of The Downliners Sect), and providing material for their excellent exhibition at Orleans House Stables Gallery, which was curated by Michele Whitby. (Michele has gone on to curate the very successful permanent Eel Pie Island Museum in York Street, Twickenham.)

We are blessed to have a group of talented and world class musicians as our house band – The Eel Pie All-Stars. They play at our (now legendary) Christmas Parties, fundraisers and other local events such as London 60s Week at The Barmy Arms on Twickenham Embankment; Strawberry Hill Music Day; Ealing Blues Festival and the Whitton 'Wish You Were Here' Festival. The Eel Pie All-Stars are Don Craine and Keith Grant of The Downliners Sect, Robin Bibi (who was a one-time member of The Pretty Things), Alan Glen (formerly with The Yardbirds and Nine Below Zero), Chris Hunt (The Dana Gillespie Band, The Bruvvers and formerly with the Lonnie Donegan Band) and Dave Lennox (who played keyboards with Blodwyn Pig).

2022 marks 'Rock's Diamond Year' – the 60-Year Anniversary of electric rhythm and blues which was kickstarted by The Ealing Club in 1962, closely followed by the Eel Pie Island Jazz Club and The Crawdaddy Club. Among many great associated events, at the Eel Pie Club we will be putting on our Cyril Davies Tribute Night with the Alan Glen/John O'Leary All-Stars featuring some of the best blues musicians in the country.

If anyone had told me back in the 1960s when I was a schoolgirl asking Arthur Chisnall if he would let me into the Eel Pie Island Jazz Club for a few meagre coppers, that I would own and run the current Eel Pie Club, I would have laughed in disbelief! I was quite a shy teenager, and not terribly confident. However, The Eel Pie Club has become my passion and now consumes my life. I have to admit that I would never have found myself owning and running The Eel Pie Club were it not for the motivation of Warren, and if it were not for the original idea and wealth of experience of the music industry passed on by our former partner, Tom Nolan. The Club also owes much of its current success to our superb Sound Technician, Doug Taylerson, our superb stage manager, John Cobb, Manager of the Cabbage Patch, Stuart Green, and our wonderful Eel Pie Club audiences. Details of all of our upcoming gigs can be found on our website at **www.eelpieclub.com** or on the Eel Pie Club Facebook page.

With fondest memories of our dear friend, Don Craine, who sadly passed away after this chapter was written.

Mud Morganfield at the Eel Pie Club, 2013. Photo: Pat Stancliffe

The original Crawdaddy Club was located at the back of The Station Hotel in Richmond. Today the building is a bar and restaurant called One Kew Road.

THE CRAWDADDY CLUB

David Sinclair

*"My favourite place, looking back, was the Station Hotel,
Richmond, just because everything really kicked off
from there."*

– Keith Richards

A grungy dance hall at the rear of the Station Hotel in Richmond
was an unlikely launch pad for the greatest rock 'n' roll band in
the world. The Rolling Stones' Sunday night residency as the
house band at the venue which became known as the Crawdaddy
Club lasted for a tumultuous seven months, from February to
September 1963. It was at one of their early gigs there that the
Stones were discovered by Andrew Loog Oldham, who would
become their manager. Oldham subsequently brought his older
business partner, the impresario Eric Easton, to see the Stones
at the Crawdaddy, an excursion which persuaded him to sign
the group, leading in short order to a recording contract with
Decca, whose A&R man, Dick Rowe, also saw them at the
Crawdaddy on May 5, 1963.

The first coverage of the Stones in the local press (*Richmond
and Twickenham Times*), the music press (*Record Mirror*) and the
national press (*Daily Mirror*) was features and reviews of them
playing at the Crawdaddy. Amid rapidly escalating crowds and
scenes of barely contained chaos, the Stones continued their

The Rolling Stones, July 1963, TV debut

weekly shows at the club following the release of their first single 'Come On' in June and first TV appearance on *Thank Your Lucky Stars* in July 1963.

In April 1963, as word of the band spread further afield, all four of the Beatles showed up to watch and hang out with the Stones at the Crawdaddy Club, the start of a lifelong camaraderie between the two most significant groups in the history of modern popular music.

Initially located at 1 Kew Road, in the Station Hotel opposite Richmond station, the Crawdaddy was (and still is) a brand as much as a venue per se. The name was invented on a whim by the promoter Giorgio Gomelsky, when a local journalist, Barry May, visited the club to see the Stones in April 1963, and asked Gomelsky what the place was called. Thinking of the Bo Diddley song 'Crawdad', which the Stones would sometimes play to close their set, Gomelsky told him it was called the Crawdaddy Club. But there was never any fixed sign for the Crawdaddy Club at the Station Hotel or at any of its subsequent incarnations at other locations.

The Station Hotel had been home to various jazz clubs since the early 1950s, but the live music scene was on the cusp of a momentous change when Gomelsky, a refugee from Soviet Georgia, who worked as a film editor at Shepperton Studios, began promoting gigs there on Sunday nights towards the end of 1962. The R&B revolution spearheaded in London by Alexis Korner and Cyril Davies and their Blues Incorporated ensemble was sweeping away the trad jazz bands who had previously ruled the roost. Gomelsky's first resident act, Dave Hunt's R&B Band – which featured guitarist Ray Davies (later of the Kinks) – was a combination of mainstream jazz and big band-style blues players.

Having seen the much harder-edged Rolling Stones play at the Red Lion in Sutton and at the Manor House in Haringey, Gomelsky hired the group to take over the residency from Dave Hunt's Band. Before the Stones' first show there on February 24, 1963, Gomelsky himself went out on a flyposting expedition on a cold winter's night with Mick Jagger, Keith Richards and Brian Jones to publicise the gig.

"The hall at the rear of the Station Hotel looked big and spare," according to James Phelge, who shared the notoriously squalid flat in Edith Grove where Jagger, Richards and Jones lived at the time, and who helped out as a roadie at local gigs. "The ceiling must have been 20-feet high above the bare wooden boards of the main floor and your footsteps echoed around the building as you walked – it sounded as if you were being followed. With all the lights on it looked even bigger than its 80 by 60 ft. size. Like all the club and pub halls it looked in need of some new paint."

Despite the flyposting campaign and an ad for the first show which Gomelsky had placed in *Melody Maker*, the turnout was somewhat disappointing (although the story that only three people turned up is a wild exaggeration that has grown over the years into an urban myth). The Stones set up on the three-foot high stage and played two sets. It was the first time that the

The Stones play the Crawdaddy Club, 1963

line-up included both Bill Wyman and Charlie Watts along with original piano player Ian Stewart. Phelge called it "an average and uninspiring evening." Others were even less impressed.

"I used to go and see the Rustics Jazz Band every week at the Station Hotel," said local music fan Heather White, better known as Fluff. "Then suddenly it was guys with guitars called the Rolling Stones. I saw their first show there and I hated them. Instead of people jiving it was people jumping up and down on the spot. I left early and went up to L'Auberge, the coffee bar nearby."

Despite the disappointing start, word of the band's new residency quickly spread. There was certainly a sizable queue outside the venue a few weeks later when Andrew Loog Oldham, a young music business wannabe who had worked as a publicist for the Beatles, ventured out to see the band. Passing two strangers – who turned out to be Mick Jagger and Chrissie Shrimpton – having an argument in the alleyway outside, Oldham made his way into "the dark and sweaty room" where, as he put it, the "hundred-odd couples seemed ready for what they were about to receive and went apeshit…"

According to Oldham, the reaction of the audience to seeing the Stones perform was nothing short of orgasmic:

"Before the pill, when sex was still a delicacy, teenagers had it artificially inseminated through vinyl and live gigs. The audience at the Station Hotel Crawdaddy Club, getting off on the Stones, were as flushed and happy as if they'd had the real thing."

Music journalist Norman Jopling, who showed up, albeit reluctantly, to review them for *Record Mirror*, also spoke with awe of the four hundred or so fans "who quickly lose all their inhibitions and proceed to contort themselves to the truly exciting music…"

As the weeks went by and word of this remarkable effect spread, the Station Hotel gradually became overwhelmed by demand to see the Stones. There were enough people queuing outside every week to fill the place before the doors even opened. Once inside, there was not enough space for people

Fans hang from the ceiling rafters at the Crawdaddy Club

to move, let alone dance, and Gomelsky instigated a one-in, one-out system allowing people to escape the crush to get outside for some fresh air, while others took their place inside. The owners became worried that the size of the audience would put them in breach of fire regulations and, having been spooked by reports of the wild nature of the shows, told Gomelsky that he would have to close the club.

The Stones played their last gig at the Station Hotel on June 16, 1963. Two weeks later the Crawdaddy re-opened half a mile down the road at the more capacious Richmond Athletic Ground in Twickenham Road, where the Stones played their first show on June 30, and where the Crawdaddy Club continues to operate to this day.

The Richmond Athletic Ground has never looked or felt much like a music venue of any sort. But even before the Stones started playing there, it had already laid one of the foundation stones of UK music culture by hosting the annual National Jazz Festival, first staged in 1961, which eventually evolved into the Reading Festival. The event was the brainchild of promoter Harold Pendleton, a former accountant and trad jazz fan who founded and ran the Marquee Club, where the Stones had played their first ever gig on July 12, 1962.

It was largely through Pendleton's vision and determination that the transition on the live circuit from traditional/Dixieland jazz to R&B and eventually modern rock was facilitated. When he staged the third National Jazz Festival at Richmond Athletic Ground in August 1963, he included the Rolling Stones on the bill – a magnanimous gesture to Gomelsky, whose Crawdaddy show with the Stones had to be cancelled that weekend.

The following year the festival became the National Jazz and Blues

THE CRAWDADDY CLUB

Festival featuring the Stones, the Yardbirds, Manfred Mann and Long John Baldry alongside Kenny Ball and his Jazzmen, the Tubby Hayes Big Band and the Ronnie Scott Quartet. After several changes of venue and musical complexion, the festival took place for the first time in Reading in 1971, where it remains to the present.

Set a long way back from the road, behind the rugby pitches where the Jazz and Blues festivals were held, the Richmond Athletic Ground clubhouse which had now become the new home of the Crawdaddy had a drab, institutional look. Inside, there was a distinct lack of atmosphere. "The first thing that struck you was how low the ceiling was," Phelge noted. "Almost to the point of being claustrophobic...The music came out the same as before, but the magic feeling of the old club was not there."

"Far too much reverence is given to the Crawdaddy in my opinion," Phelge has insisted in hindsight. "It only had prominence when the Stones played there while it was located at the Station Hotel. It was crap after it moved to the Athletic ground which seems to have hijacked or had the glory of the real club thrust upon it. Even the Stones couldn't generate the same fever pitch atmosphere there as they had done before."

Others remember it differently. David Cressy, who was a 17-year-old Hammersmith schoolboy and a regular at the Crawdaddy in 1963, noted in his diary: "To Crawdaddy to see Stones – packed, hot sweaty room yes – exciting, violent, shaking, stimulating, exhibitive enjoyment." In the excitement at one of the gigs there, Cressy lost his shirt, which he retrieved during the interval from the Stones' dressing room. "The group were all drinking rum and blackcurrant, listening to 45s, including 'Poison Ivy', on a portable gramophone," he remembered. "They were incredibly polite and helpful and used the turntable as a desk to sign a publicity photo – so the autographs are somewhat shaky."

One of Cressy's school friends, Ray Lipton, got a job in Giorgio Gomelsky's office at 18 Carlisle Street in Soho and kept his mates well informed of developments. Once the Stones had departed on a schedule of national and international tours, Gomelsky wasted no time filling the vacancy for a house band at the Crawdaddy with another up-and-coming, local R&B group, the Yardbirds. Less than a month after their first gig at the venue, their lead guitarist Top Topham left to be replaced in October 1963 by an 18-year-old, ex-Kingston College art student called Eric Clapton.

THE YARDBIRDS

Like the Stones before them, the Yardbirds' reputation as a live act spread like wildfire. Paul Stokes, who nowadays plays drums in the Crawdaddy Blues Band (named in honour of the club), became a hardcore fan of the Yardbirds and saw them play many times at the Crawdaddy. "They were simply the greatest band I ever saw," Stokes said. "Incredible songs and stage presence. And it was an amazing scene at the Crawdaddy. You often saw people from other groups down there. I was watching the Yardbirds once and Brian Jones wandered out of the dressing room." There is a celebrated picture of Stokes

L-R: Jeff Beck, Jim McCarty, Chris Dreja, Jimmy Page,Keith Relf. Photo M.Ochs

hanging upside down from one of the RSJs above the crowd on the dancefloor at one of the Yardbirds gigs at the Crawdaddy.

Gomelsky soon became the Yardbirds' manager and secured them a recording contract with Columbia Records. Gomelsky's assistant Hamish Grimes, who designed all the marketing and promotional materials for the Crawdaddy, invented a typeface and a distinctive hipster lingo which he used for advertising both the group and the venue. You can hear Grimes introducing the band at the start of their debut LP, *Five Live Yardbirds*: "Good evening, and welcome, and now it is time for birdmarising, yardmarising, in fact most blueswailing Yardbirds…"

That album released in December 1964 was recorded across town at the Marquee. But a year before that, on December 8, 1963, the band teamed up with visiting American blues legend Sonny Boy Williamson to record a live album at the Crawdaddy *Sonny Boy Williamson & The Yardbirds*.

Throughout 1964, the Crawdaddy under the reign of Gomelsky and Grimes was a vehicle for promoting the Yardbirds almost as much as it was a venue. They also began putting on regular gigs under the Crawdaddy banner at other venues as far afield as the Star Hotel in Croydon and Staines Rugby Club in Hanworth. On March 14, the box ad which the venue took out in the Gig Guide section of *Record Mirror* proclaimed:

CRAWDADDY R&B

It started 80 weeks ago with the Rolling Stones in Richmond, the centre of R&B. It is now the most raving R&B club in Britain, with the most blueswailing, fan-followed YARDBIRDS who give forth

Every Sunday – RAA grounds, Richmond.

Every Wednesday and Saturday at the Star Hotel, London Road, Croydon.

Come and feel the sound!!

As the year went on and the increasing demands on the Yardbirds' schedule impacted on their availability, Gomelsky filled the Crawdaddy's date sheet with residencies by other R&B groups including the T-Bones from Sussex, fronted by singer Gary Farr; the Moody Blues, a Birmingham band

Sugar Pie DeSanto

T-Bone Walker, Hamburg, 1972. Photo: Heinrich Klaffs

with London management; the Authentics featuring a young session guitarist called Jimmy Page; and organist Brian Auger, who played harpsichord on the Yardbirds' breakthrough single 'For Your Love', and went on to front his own band the Trinity with Julie Driscoll.

Now in its pomp, the Crawdaddy also attracted visiting American blues stars including Little Walter, Jimmy Reed, T-Bone Walker and Sugar Pie DeSanto, the female blues shouter from San Francisco, whose performances incorporated wild dancing and even a standing backflip.

As well as attending to his usual promotional duties, Grimes is said to have taken the unorthodox initiative of spreading the new musical gospel by means of a graffiti campaign proclaiming 'Clapton is God'. "I've always suspected he was the one who went out there with a pot of paint and a brush and painted that on the wall," Clapton told *Classic Rock* magazine in 2016.

God had left the band by the time the Yardbirds' single 'For Your Love' entered the UK pop chart in March 1965. 'Concrashyoulations to the Yardbirds from Crawdaddy' blared the venue's ad in *Record Mirror*, as the song continued on its way to a No.3 peak in the UK (and later No.6 in the US.) With their new guitarist, 20-year-old Jeff Beck – previously with Chiswick-based band the Tridents – the Yardbirds played their last Sunday show at the Crawdaddy on June 27, 1965.

Not long after, in August, came news of the Crawdaddy's first shutdown. The message was delivered in Yardbirdspeak:

"The powers that be, down Richmond lerkin' round the A.A. grounds don't like music or anybody, so they closed us. It's a shame after 3 years, but we shall reopen... someplace else...soon..."

"The excuse was that the Crown Commission would not give permission for the lease," Grimes explained to the *NME*. "But I understand unruly behaviour of a few members was another reason."

The Crawdaddy continued to stage gigs in Croydon until September 1965. But Gomelsky's priority at this point was managing the Yardbirds, among several other projects, and as the band's international profile rapidly expanded, so his interest in promoting the Crawdaddy languished.

The Richmond Athletic Ground was revived as a venue somewhat in the late 1960s when various promoters used it on an ad hoc basis to put on bands. It became the go-to location for the Isleworth Polytechnic Students Union to put on acts who were too popular (or expensive) to be accommodated in their own SU hall at Spring Grove House in London Road. Beginning with a show by the Pretty Things in early 1967, acts that are known to have played at Richmond Athletic Ground included Bluesology (the band led by Long John Baldry with Reg Dwight aka Elton John on keyboards), the Brian Auger Trinity with Julie Driscoll, Pink Floyd (for whose show the venue was renamed the Middle Earth); and an early appearance in 1968 by Led Zeppelin (who had only recently stopped billing themselves as the New Yardbirds).

"The publicity may have said 'Isleworth Polytechnic presents...' or whoever was promoting, but we all still knew it as the Crawdaddy," said singer and harmonica player John Habes, who was on the Student Union entertainments committee at Isleworth (now West Thames College). "It was a monthly thing for about two years. We charged 5/ – or 7/6 for a ticket, and the shows were always sold out. I remember when I wasn't on the SU anymore, I went there to see Peter Green's Fleetwood Mac with my girlfriend – who is now my wife – and we couldn't get in. It was so hot, they opened the doors, so we stood and listened to them outside."

In the mid-1990s the Crawdaddy Club enjoyed a slight return at its original location, the Station Hotel, when singer and guitarist Ian McHugh – now host of the weekly podcast *Blues Is The Truth* – organised a Tuesday-night jam session and, along with singer and guitarist Will Johns and others, started booking acts under the Crawdaddy banner.

But it was not until March 2, 2012, that the spirit of '63 was invoked once more, when local music fan and part-time impresario Mike Rivers, re-launched the Crawdaddy as

Bluesology with Reg Dwight (Elton John) on the right

a monthly club event at the Richmond Athletic Ground. Bill Wyman showed up for a grand opening night performance by local R&B favourites the Blue Bishops.

The revived Crawdaddy has now been running for 10 years, a success story which Rivers attributes to the great history of the venue and the continuing power of its musical legacy. He cites two sold-out shows by blues chanteuse Jo Harman as his pick of many memorable gigs since he took on the job.

Singer Paul Stewart and his band the Others from Hampton Grammar School, who played at the Crawdaddy on multiple occasions during the Gomelsky era, have reformed and returned to play the Crawdaddy several times during the Rivers incarnation of the club. "What's interesting is that quite a lot of the people there are the same people as the first time around," Stewart says. "It's just that they, like we, have got older. What Mike Rivers has managed to do is create a very similar atmosphere, I think. It's not as frenetic as it was – there's no more swinging off the RSJ beams – and it's nowhere near as full as in the old days. But a tremendous musical legacy has been preserved and celebrated."

The Others, 1964

The Richmond Athletic Ground today

Mick Jagger *(left)*, Charlie Watts *(centre)* Giorgio Gomelsky, *(right)*,
backstage at Wembley, 1964
Photo: Jeremy Fletcher

IGNITION – GIORGIO GOMELSKY

Cheryl Robson

"Kepler said that "the only constant in the universe is change" and change is scary sometimes. I like to believe that the purpose of art is that of making change less fearful so we can face it with more joy than pain, with more information and less confusion, and celebrate this mysterious state of "being alive" to its fullest."
– Giorgio Gomelsky

One mysterious name that crops up in accounts of musicians talking about the music scene around Richmond in the 1960s is that of Giorgio Gomelsky. He was a mover and shaker who had a hand in many different aspects of the music industry in the UK, Europe and the US, from running music clubs, to producing records to managing bands, but his quixotic nature and disdain for business matters hampered his success.

How did a Georgian-born refugee whose family fled the Stalinist purges in the Soviet Union, end up in war-torn Italy, and become a kind of musical provocateur for rock 'n' roll? The experience of cultural dislocation changed him:

"I listened a lot – when you can't speak you become a listener."

As a boy hiding with friends during the German Occupation, they found and played some old Jazz records in an attic which inspired his love of the genre. As a teen he voraciously read the *Melody Maker* and the *Cahiers du Jazz*, listened to jazz on the radio, and to pursue his passion further, he would hitchhike or cycle around Europe with friends, visiting jazz clubs in Germany and Italy. In Paris, he had the good fortune to see Charlie Parker play.

In his 20s, receiving a small inheritance, he organised a jazz festival at a disused airbase in Ancona, Switzerland, where he had previously gone to a Benedictine school. In 1954, he formed a Swiss federation of jazz societies and tried to stage a street concert as part of the Zurich Festival. Despite resistance from the city elders, his staging of a street protest that involved a lot of young people mooning, persuaded them to allow the concert to go ahead, and consequently a jazz festival later sprang up in Zurich (founded by André Berne) which continues to this day.

Gomelsky's mother was a successful French hat designer for Claude Saint-Cyr, and when she moved to London to set up a new atelier, Gomelsky followed her, intent on pursuing a career in filmmaking. Arriving in London in 1955, he set

Poster for the Zurich JazzNoJazz Festival 2018

IGNITION – GIORGIO GOMELSKY

The Rolling Stones playing at the National Jazz Festival, 1964

up a coffee bar off the King's Road that attracted hip young people to hang out and listen to the new music. Chris Barber and Johnny Dankworth were within his circle, attracted by Gomelsky's knowledge and enthusiasm for jazz. Gomelsky had made short documentary films and offered his services as a volunteer to Harold Pendleton who was organising the first National Jazz Festival. He built relationships with the National Jazz Federation too, persuading them to let him film the next festival in 1960. He wrote reviews for *Jazz News* and although he wanted to make a film about the more experimental Dankworth, Pendleton persuaded him to film the more traditional Chris Barber performing at the Royal Festival Hall. Times were changing, and the emerging trend for electric R&B soon grabbed his attention.

"When I got to London in the mid-fifties, the "pop" scene was just a pale imitation of white US commercial music. At least there was a local "do-it-yourself" music, "skiffle", (imported to the UK by British bandleader Chris Barber) derived from Lonnie Johnson and other blues/folksters, which allowed young people to take up instruments."[i]

i. i Giorgio Gomelsky interview. https://www.eurock.com/features/giorgio.aspx

Chris Barber persuaded Pendleton, who had recently opened the Marquee Club as a jazz venue, to give over Thursday nights to the electric blues and soon bands like Blues Incorporated began to gig there. When the Rolling Stones played there, their version of blues classics didn't go down too well, and Cyril Davies asked the band to leave. With his boundless energy, Gomelsky then initiated the first London R&B Festival at a club in Ham Yard lining up Blues Incorporated, Blues by Six and the nascent Rolling Stones to perform. Finding it hard to attract audiences to central London during the week, and not wanting to compete with the Marquee, he looked towards the well-heeled western suburbs where the Ealing Club was already operating successfully attracting crowds of young people to the new electric R&B sound.

L'Auberge in Richmond was a popular haunt for young people at the time and understanding that public transport was key to getting an audience, Gomelsky persuaded the manager of the Station Hotel to let him use a room at the back of the building on Sunday nights. Right opposite the station, his new R&B club opened with the Dave Hunt band and when they departed, he booked the Rolling Stones, encouraging them to play popular covers of songs by the American blues greats such as Muddy Waters and Howlin' Wolf. They'd finish their set with a lively rendition of Bo Diddley's song 'Crawdad' which would set the audience on fire.

To help bring in an audience, he persuaded the local news to cover the gigs and enticed a few music critics to venture out to Richmond to review the band. The great coverage he achieved in the press put the club on the map, but it outraged the brewery and Gomelsky found himself evicted, having to set up down the road in a room at the Richmond Athletic Ground which had far less ambience and thinner acoustics. He was promoting and managing the Rolling Stones for almost a year before the arrival of Andrew Loog Oldham on the scene. Gomelsky felt "tremendously let down" by the group's

Five Live Yardbirds album

decision to move on as he had been away in Switzerland for a few weeks making arrangements for his father's funeral.

He soon bounced back and got his teeth into managing the Yardbirds, booking a US tour backing Sonny Boy Williamson, and bringing out a joint live album recorded at the Crawdaddy in December 1963. With an understanding of fonts and design, he even sketched out the band's logo which was used on all their posters and merchandising, perhaps the first time a band was marketed with its own branding. Then he had a hand in producing the *Five Live Yardbirds* album, having signed the group to EMI's Columbia label. Although it contained their most popular live number, a cover of Howlin' Wolf's 'Smokestack Lightning', the record found little success at the time; later critics credited its improvisational style as laying the foundations for groups like Cream.

In 1964 Gomelsky also organised the first British R&B Festival in Birmingham, featuring the Yardbirds, Long John Baldry and the Spencer Davis Group among others. He encouraged the Yardbirds to experiment with exotic instruments and Gregorian chants and to record 'For Your Love', the Graham Gouldman song, which became a Top 3 hit in 1965. Despite the success of this record, the group would move on to manager Simon Napier-Bell in 1967.

The roster of bands that Gomelsky booked at the Crawdaddy, including the Moody Blues and Led Zeppelin, proved an exciting mix of the hottest young bands in the country and the success of the venue enabled him to get backing for his own record label. In 1966, he established Marmalade records which was distributed by Polydor and backed by Deutsche Gramophone. Alongside this, he was managing a design company, building a recording studio and managing numerous other bands. Not only that but he was constantly liaising with European counterparts and creating a kind of touring circuit to Europe for British bands. In a flurry of activity, he released over 20 singles and over a dozen albums in the space of three years. The most successful act on the Marmalade label was Julie Driscoll, Brian Auger & the Trinity. Her recording of the Dylan track 'This Wheel's on Fire' reached No 5 in the charts in 1968. But by the end of 1969, tastes in music were changing, Gomelsky was spread too thinly over too many projects, and the record company had burned through its funds. His backers pulled out and Gomelsky began to look for pastures new.

Returning to Paris in 1970 to escape what he called the "perfidious Albions", he intended to focus on filmmaking but when an interviewer asked for his opinion of a new experimental band called Magma, he was hooked again by the

Magma performing at Roadburn Festival, 2017
Photo: Grywnn

progressive sounds he heard – a fusion of blues, jazz, classical, rock and pop and lyrics sung in a strange language.

> "I had never heard anything like it. I was very impressed by their "sources" and their musical skills. This was not run-of-the-mill stuff. It also wasn't "commercial" by any stretch of the imagination. But I'm a sucker for underdogs, so I was tempted to take on the challenge."[ii]

Recognising the talent of Christian Vander and his group, he started to manage Magma, and discovered that he could book them into youth centres across the country on a very favorable box office split basis. In this way he built a network of venues and with youth audiences of around 200 teenagers at each show, he gradually built a new fan base for the band.

He was able to sign Magma to A&M Records and got them into the recording studio that Richard Branson had set up in a manor house at the village of Shipton-on-Cherwell in Oxfordshire, where Tubular Bells had been recorded the year before. There, Gomelsky produced their groundbreaking concept album Mëkanïk Dëstruktïẁ Kömmandöh, known as MDK. A&M didn't fully appreciate the work and refused to release the original album but on May 6th 1973 a version was finally released that became a self-styled genre known as "zeuhl." The French edition of *Rolling Stone* magazine would later list the album as the 33rd greatest French rock album of all time and in 2015, they ranked the album 24th on their list of the '50 Greatest Prog Rock Albums of All Time'.

Soon Magma were playing to audiences of 3000-5000 people and their *Live* (at the Olympia) double album sold 150,000 copies in France alone. The band were invited to play at Newport Jazz festival in the USA, a rare accolade for a French group. Magma became a hugely influential creative force in French music in the late 70s and were commercially successful too but, perhaps inevitably, internal squabbles split the band and Gomelsky bailed out.

i. ii Giorgio Gomelsky interview https://www.eurock.com/features/giorgio.aspx

During this period, Gomelsky met and married Brigitte Guichard, (their marriage was later dissolved) as well as creating a new management company called Rock Pas Dégénéré which grew to become one of the main talent agencies in France. He took on bands from other countries and created an international touring circuit across Europe building audiences for new music.

In Paris he also reconnected with Australian beatnik Daevid Allen of Soft Machine who, due to visa problems, could not get back to the UK after a French tour.

"I always felt bad for him because I was the one who in the summer of 1968 had sent them to St Tropez (a holiday resort in the South of France) to play in a club and get their stuff together. When they [Soft Machine] came back to the UK, Daevid, an Australian citizen, was refused entrance, so he had to return to Paris where he started Gong!"[iii]

He helped to develop Gong, getting them a gig at the Glastonbury Festival and then a three-record deal with Virgin records. The band went through various incarnations; original member and poet Gilli Smyth recalls:

"The original Gong band was like a magic mushroom that had grown too large, spawned a series of mushrooms and when it blew apart in the wind all its members went off to develop their own particular vision."[iv]

On receipt of a large royalty cheque for the Yardbirds, Gomelsky moved to New York in 1978 and leased a mid-town loft which became a popular hang out for musicians and artists, like his friend Jean-Michel Basquiat. He recorded a Gong album and staged a concert featuring dozens of bands, which quickly sold out.

Not realising the challenges of working in the US, Gomelsky booked a US tour for Gong to play 33 gigs spread out across the country and they set off in an old school bus, but the tour was a disaster and they returned home broke and disillusioned.

He worked as a DJ at Tramps nightclub and allowed the ground floor of his building in Chelsea to be used as a rehearsal studio for many bands such as Jeff Buckley. He discovered hiphop artists, and inspired new wave rock bands such as Bill Laswell's Material. Wherever he went, he had a nose for the coming thing and seemed to act as a catalyst for experimentation, the blue touch paper for something new and authentic.

"I was always digging for something that didn't exist," he said. His desire to push the envelope inspired many but was often at odds with those in the music business, whose main motivation was either fame or money. For Gomelsky, it was all about the music and communicating with audiences. Without his eccentricity and entrepreneurialism, SW London might never have been the launchpad for rock legends that it is today.

Musician Marc Campbell described him thus:

"He was impossible to lie to. He had a bullshit detector that could not be evaded. When my band, The Nails, got signed to RCA, Giorgio warned me of the dangers of getting carried away by the lure of power and possible fame. He hated the major music corporations (he had worked at RCA) and the way they had reduced rock and roll to a mere commodity. He gave me the same advice he gave The Rolling Stones: "Don't do it for the money, do it for love." [v]

Gomelsky died of cancer on 13 January 2016 in New York City.

i.v https://dangerousminds.net/comments/the_mad_genius_behind_the_rolling_stones_and_yardbirds_giorgio_gomelsky

Gomelsky NYC, 2009
Photo: Wwwhatsup

The Bull's Head Pub, Barnes
Photo: Edwardx

THE BULL'S HEAD

Interview with Pete Feenstra

When did you first go to the Bull's Head?

It was 1971 when I first went there. I saw several bands including Barbara Thompson & Art Themen (Saxes), also separately, guitarist Terry Smith and vibes player Bill Le Sage.

Was it a jazz venue when you first went there?

Yes, 99% jazz, but it veered towards "Modern Jazz" with people like Tubby Hayes, Tommy Whittle, Dick Morrissey (with Martin Drew drums, Tony Archer bass) and the more old-school legends like John Chilton and Humphrey Lyttelton. Also Bobby Wellins, Don Weller, Terry Smith, Tony Lee, Alan Skidmore etc., and American guests like Sonny Stitt, Roy Eldridge and Johnny Griffin. Occasionally there were also American blues-related guests like Jimmy Witherspoon and Mark Murphy.

Do you know how it started/who started it?

Albert and Betty Tolley started there in 1959 about a month after the opening of Ronnie Scott's Club and by 1967 it was: "A seven-days-a-week venue with a Modern Jazz policy."

Which was the most memorable band you saw?

Just in terms of the atmosphere, musical brilliance and charisma I'd say former Frank Zappa drummer and singer Jimmy Carl Black & The Muffin Men.

Other memorable nights included "An Evening of Jacques Brel" with Alan Clayson – probably the only time the old jazz room was dominated by French fans.

The Times favourably reviewed Australian box-blues guitarist Fiona Boyes, while Finnish slide guitarist Erja Lyyinen also gained a 5 star review in the prestigious *The Blues* magazine.

UK blues guitarist Ian Parker remarkably filled the room during one of the biggest rainstorms in 20 years, while American blues guitarist Carvin Jones played a sold out 3-month residency, which we sometimes extended to two Mondays a month. He is an incredible performer, playing two guitars simultaneously while walking round the room. I very much doubt the old venue has ever seen his like since.

There was also New Jersey's Billy Walton Band, with a magnificent horns section.

Did you ever play there yourself?

No, but I promoted bands there for years and reviewed a number of shows there.

Any funny stories?

I do recall that Mick Jagger and his huge security guy had to spend time in the Thai restaurant as there wasn't – and still isn't – a dressing room for musicians.

Come the second set, Mick was still next door. So his brother Chris Jagger asked "Where's my brother?" and having paused for thought, he said something like, "Of course he had to skip off and use his OAP bus pass."

Another time Mick Waller (former Rod Stewart/Long John Baldry/John Mayall drummer etc) turned up at the venue dripping wet in shorts from the London to Brighton bike rally and jumped straight behind his drum kit to play the first set of the evening.

When I started there, there was a long-standing doorman called Don, who would be there six months of the year, while

The ABC & D of Boogie Woogie, 2010. Photo: Poiseon Bild & Text

spending the other six months in Miami. He didn't seem to like much of the music, even a lot of the Jazz, and he actually used to fall asleep at the door. Then there was also a genial Irishman who ran the music room bar when they actually opened it. He was a very droll, but lovely guy, who I later discovered was about 92!

The evening of the ABC & D of Boogie Woogie was followed by an impromptu jam with Roger Chapman and Axel Zwingenberger and all sorts of guests. It was the one and only time the venue allowed music after hours to my knowledge.

I saw at least two quite well-known musicians fall off the stage, worse for wear, – not an easy task given the small height of the stage!

Back in the early 90s I was asked to do some PR for The Chiswick Flyovers, a hard-hitting R&B band – a bit like The Pirates meets the original Dr. Feelgood. They wanted to do the Bull's Head, and get some publicity.

I was apprehensive about the whole thing. Needless to say they barely got into the second number of the sound check, when they were summarily told to stop and leave. On one occasion, the guv'nor of the Bull's Head refused to put *The Times* music correspondent on the guest list to review ABC & D of Boogie Woogie. It took all my experience to sort the problem. We duly got a great review.

Which bands did you book to play there?

I've been promoting for over 40 years, including 20 years at the Boom Boom Club in Sutton, and major London venues like Shepherds Bush Empire and Bottom Line, The Mean Fiddler and The Fairfield Halls in Croydon.

At the Bull's Head I ran the "Stormy Monday Club" with the late George McFall for 20 years. I successfully transferred the annual Junior Wells Memorial Show to Barnes and booked the John O'Leary (Savoy Brown founder member) and Alan Glen

L-R: John O'Leary, (voc/harp), Papa George (voc/gtr), Pete Miles (drums), Glynn Evans (bass), Nick Newall (sax/flute), Alan Glen (gtr/voc), Tim Penn (piano)

(Yardbirds/9 Below Zero) house band to establish the monthly 'Back to The Flamingo' residency. It started on 26 September 2011 and became one of London's most established big band residencies. The band also included former Kinks and John Mayall sax player Nick Newall, veteran Australian drummer Pete Miles and keyboard player Tim Penn. The band ended up playing an all-star Shepherds Bush Empire benefit show for Walter Trout.

We could attract tour bands and special guests as Monday was often a night off for bands. I focused mainly on blues, R&B occasionally jazz and even promoted Balkan folk music.

Notable gigs: The ABC & D of Boogie Woogie with Axel Zwingenberger, Ben Waters, Charlie Watts, Dave Green, Jools Holland, Hugh Laurie, Chris Jagger etc, which was billed as part of The London Jazz Festival.

Chris and Mick Jagger's acoustic duo; Ronnie Wood with Ben Waters and friends, and Carvin Jones (USA) 3-month residency, which attracted sell-out shows, special guests and media.

I also established two other monthly residencies with England test cricketer Mark Butcher and one with Mike Berry (60s pop star/actor).

There was also a remarkable American band called The Former Members featuring David Bennett Cohen, Greg Douglass, Roy Blumenfeld and Bruce Bartholl. It was probably the first gig where the music was interspersed with countless stories, a format which is nowadays commonplace with heritage artists of all genres.

There was a completely different jazz audience for Memphis -born, New Orleans pianist Charlie Wood, and a roomful of Americana fans along with Nick Lowe and Elvis Costello's original manager Jake Rivera, for the "titan of the telecaster", Bill Kirchen, who made his name with Commander Cody & The Lost Planet Airmen.

Entrance to the music venue

The space has changed – has this changed the ambience and/or acoustics?

Yes, it completely changed the gig. The ambience is totally different; the stage is half the size and the bar, if ever open, is tiny. The ambience of the original space was described by the academic Katherine Williams in a paper called 'Valuing Jazz':

"Like Ronnie Scott's there was no dance floor. Combined with the rows of seating the focus was on listening to the music."

In America, specialised jazz clubs such as Birdland, the Village Vanguard and the Blue Note have a similar aesthetic. From my perspective, this could be both a help and a hindrance. The very formal layout made access to seats difficult, and the above comment is right, as it was all about keeping people focused.

Which bands have made recordings at the venue?

Not many. There was always a problem with this because the management priced projects out of existence, so we settled on videoing some gigs, especially The Flamingo Nights.

It's near to the Olympic Studios in Barnes – was there any crossover?

Some musicians would come in for a drink (after they'd already been in The Sun pub round the corner) and on occasions jam. People like Bobby Tench (Jeff Beck/Van Morrison/Streetwalkers etc) would frequently drop by, but in reality most of the famous musicians belonged to the Barnes Bowls Club because it had an all-day private members license.

Anything else you'd like to add?

It's always been a bit of a jazz outpost (ie a SW London suburban venue which survived by having a booking tie-in with Ronnie Scott's. It wasn't really on a lot of people's gig circuit until the noughties. I suspect the venue liked it that way. It had a certain ambience in which history hung heavily. Even after the change in smoking policy, the old room had a dark and very traditional feel, from the seating arrangement and the black and white photos on the wall, to the Youngs real ale. The fact that the brewery tried to sell it off before it was rescued by Humphrey Lyttelton and Tim Rice etc speaks volumes about the struggle to keep it going.

I think it's always been implicitly recognised that the Bull's Head was different to other venues, being a seated layout with the emphasis on listening. For me, this meant booking more acoustic oriented artists and residencies. In that respect you could say the old venue's traditions have lived on.

Left to right: The late Bob Bonsey (doorman) Demarcus Sumter (drums), Pete Feenstra (promoter) Eliza Neals (vocalist), Howard Glazer (guitar)

The Half Moon Pub, Putney

THE HALF MOON

Patrick Humphries

If any one public house merits the phrase "musicians' pub", it's this Young's public house on the Lower Richmond Road in Putney. Over the years it's played host to everyone from Kate Bush to Kasabian. There is something cosy and welcoming which makes it a regular haunt for performers who live in and around that corner of South West London, and back in the day, you could find Bert Jansch or Ralph McTell propping up the bar.

Putney itself was listed in the Domesday Book and by the 18th Century had become one of the most fashionable of the London suburbs.

Early on in the 1960s, the area was swept up by the R&B boom which gained a foothold around Eel Pie Island. Gerry Lockran, Royd Rivers and Cliff Aungier started to host live music in the back room of the Half Moon pub in 1963. Alexis Korner, who played in many of the clubs in the area, was a regular at 'the Moon' too. Visiting Americans such as Sonny Terry & Brownie McGee, Mose Allison and Arthur 'Big Boy' Crudup sometimes played at the venue too. A 60s handbill for 'Club Folksville' at the Half Moon also featured Long John Baldry ("fantastic blues star and poll-winning singer").

It's rumoured that the Rolling Stones played the venue soon after the Half Moon started hosting gigs in 1963, but I have been unable to find any record of them appearing. The band, however, did hire the Half Moon for a private event in 2000.

A press report on Thursday 4th May ran:

"The Rolling Stones were in the Half Moon Pub in Putney Southwest London, UK last night, for a memorial/tribute to Joe Seabrook, Keith Richards' personal assistant for the last few years. Joe died prematurely on 31 March, and this night was an event for him. It started at 6pm, and Keith Richards, arrived at 6:10pm, looking really cool in a green shirt and long black overcoat. Next to arrive was Charlie, dressed as always in an immaculate suit. Then Ronnie arrived and after much speculation, Mick Jagger appeared at about 8pm. It was a private function, closed to the public, with about 300 people in attendance. Keith and Ronnie played on stage with the hired band, playing 4 old blues /rock 'n' roll standards, but unfortunately Mick and Charlie didn't perform".

The territory was also rich in folk clubs – Kingston's Barge, Richmond's Hanging Lamp. Twickenham's The Crown. The Half Moon seemed to act as a magnet to the cream of the British folk-rock movement – the Strawberry Hill Boys ("famous country music trio") who were soon to metamorphose into the Strawbs. John Martyn, Roy Harper, Ralph McTell, John Renbourn, Bert Jansch, Richard Thompson were only some who were given house room at the Moon during the 1960s and 70s. Fairport Convention used to use the pub as a warm-up venue for their annual Cropredy reunion.

On entering the Half Moon, pausing for a pint at the bar, you made your way through to the music room. There were few tables and no seats, and the capacity was estimated at around 250, though for the bigger names, it was almost certainly exceeded. Much of the atmosphere was generated by the venue's compere, the late Johnny 'Jonah' Jones.

THE HALF MOON

Ralph McTell *(centre)* Saloon Bar, Half Moon, Putney. Photo: Dave Peabody

Musician and photographer Dave Peabody recalls:

"The date was Thursday 27th March 1986. American singer-songwriters Jerry Jeff Walker, who wrote 'Mr. Bojangles', and Guy Clark were booked to play a double bill at the Half Moon, Putney and I had gone along to listen and take a few photos. At the gig's finish, the audience were ushered out of the music room while compere Johnny Jones took Gerry, Guy and myself around to the saloon bar. Along with a few of the pub's regulars, we were permitted a "lock-in" by the landlord and drinks began to flow. At some unannounced point, the improvised quartet of Gerry, Guy, Johnny and me, spontaneously burst into a full-throated acappella rendition of 'Goodnight, Irene', much to the amazement of all in attendance. Johnny Jones, who had never before been heard to utter a single musical note, gave as good, and sung just as heartily, as the rest of us. Ah… the power of Young's Ale and the magic of the Half Moon."

The Balham Alligators at the Half Moon, Putney, 1987. Photo: Dave Peabody
L-R: Geraint Watkins, Robin McKidd, Kieron O'Connor, Pete Dennis, Gary Rickard

I've spent many a happy evening there too and among the most memorable were watching the Home Service, the sadly short-lived folk 'supergroup' which arose from the ashes of the Albion Band… Ex-Bonzo Dog Doo-Dah Band member Bob Kerr with his Whoopee Band. Among the legendary performers were also Memphis Slim and Stephane Grappelli and the world's best-named banjoist – Vernon Dudley Bohay-Nowell … Another splinter group, the GPs, with ex-Fairporters Richard Thompson, Dave Pegg and Dave Mattacks aided by Ralph McTell, pumping out high-energy rock 'n' roll covers.

Declan Macmanus was another Half Moon regular. Later to take his mother's maiden name and the Christian name of the late lamented King of Rock 'n' Roll, Elvis Costello was onstage twice a month during the mid-70s. Charlie Dore witnessed him in action "He was intense, utterly focused… He didn't suffer fools gladly". Soon after Declan signed to Stiff Records.

Funnily enough, while Pub Rock was keeping mid-70s pub landlords and brewers happy, the Half Moon didn't play much of a part. Dr Feelgood certainly played there, but mostly the pub rockers concentrated on pubs nearer the centre, like Earl's Court's The Nashville or Camden's Hope & Anchor.

The Half Moon picked up on the 'comedy is the new rock 'n' roll' scene of the late 80s and early 90s – Harry Hill, Sean Hughes, Jack Whitehall and Al Murray all played there. As did their 'Godfather' Billy Connolly. The Big Yin had, after all, begun life in the folk duo the Humblebums alongside Gerry Rafferty, where he got to know many of the luminaries of the folk scene.

Legend has it that after a gig at the Moon, Connolly was driven home by his mate Ralph McTell, only to get completely lost. "For fuck's sake, Ralph," observed his passenger, "you wrote 'Streets Of London'!"

July 1980 was a date which entered the Half Moon's history: U2 were playing their second gig there, and it became a landmark for the Irish quartet, marking the first time they'd ever sold out a UK venue!

By the 1980s, you never knew who you might bump into – at the height of Dire Straits' success, Mark Knopfler joined Paul Brady on the pub stage. The Moon was able to attract names like Del Shannon, Nick Cave and Taj Mahal. The much-loved Balham Alligators were regulars. Alt-country diva k.d.lang made her UK debut there, and a teenage Kate Bush was there with the KT Bush Band a few years prior to 'Wuthering Heights'. A young Ed Sheeran also trod the boards.

Like many of the London pubs, the Half Moon was feeling the pinch, and by 2010 there were rumours that it would be closed permanently. However, a petition of 6,500 names (including many of the musicians who'd played there) halted its closure, and happily, on into its seventh decade is still one of the key London venues to showcase new acts.

These days, on many nights, the Half Moon plays host to tribute bands – giving us a taste of the originals you'd love to have seen back in those heady days of the 60s – The Beatles, Rolling Stones, Traveling Wilburys, REM, Led Zeppelin…

Music historian, the late John Platt, in his book *London's Rock Routes*, called the Half Moon "one of the friendliest atmospheres of any London venue". Today, the Half Moon can lay claim to being one of the longest-running live music venues in London and R&B is still on the bill, with artists like Dave Kelly (co-founder of the Blues Band with Paul Jones) playing his distinctive brand of blues and roots music to a multigenerational crowd.

THE HALF MOON

Canadian singer-songwriter K.D.Lang with banjo, c. 2014

Clewer Mead, Windsor, 1967

GETTING ON DOWN TO RICKY-TICK CLUBS

Pete Clack

"Everybody I spoke to that went to the Ricky-Tick said they had a magical time. It was a privilege to be there because you could see mega-artists for 50p."

– John Mansfield

One day quite recently, my son said to me, being himself a big live music fan, "Dad, you saw all those great bands live, before they hit the world, you were just so fortunate." I had to totally agree with him, mostly thanks to visiting Ricky-Tick Clubs, and enjoy-ing those incredible nights, with fantastic artists many of whom would become true music legends. You had to be there to have the memories of just how special it was, but I hope I can give you just a small flavour of those times as I recall them myself. It all seems like yesterday, which in some ways it really was!

In his recent autobiography, Stevie Van Zandt (E Street Band) said the best music was in the 60s, because by the time the 70s came along everything was being mixed in the studio so much that the spirit of the original music was choked. The true live sounds were gone because of the way record producers were trying to make everything sound perfect and the real music was lost in a cave of over-production.

The Ricky-Tick clubs were set up by co-founders John Mansfield and Philip Hayward after they saw the success of the Ealing Club back in 1962. They became incredibly influential in the R&B and soul scenes of the 60s and 70s. A night at a Ricky-Tick Club would leave you with lifelong memories of just how great live music could be and it always came at an affordable price too! Mansfield and Hayward developed the Ricky-Tick Clubs to promote new music and live bands, bringing so many new artists to the fore who would go on to become huge stars in later years, and in many cases they are still up there, still producing creative and exciting music today.

The night just after his debut television appearance with *Hey Joe,* I remember seeing Jimi Hendrix live for the first time, and where else but at a Ricky-Tick Club? Others during that time included Cream, Zoot Money's Big Roll Band, Pink Floyd, the Rolling Stones, John Mayall's Bluesbreakers, the Pretty Things, The Who, and the man who always packed anywhere he played – Geno Washington and his Ram Jam Band. Another favourite was Chris Farlowe and the Thunderbirds, plus the woefully underrated Julian Covey and His Machine, and last but not least, Them (Van Morrison's band at the time who produced pop hits such as *Baby Please Don't Go* and *Here Comes The Night,* before Van went solo and created his own musical history).

I was so taken with Southampton's Simon Dupree and The Big Sound (along with their horn section) that after seeing the band play at Ricky-Tick I rushed out the next day to grab a copy of their new single. After a few drinks I went upstairs on the bus to return home, dropped my new single, which unfortunately cracked so I had to go back and buy another one the following day. At least I still have that record now, it's just a lot more worn over the years. There were so many fantastic bands around back then that I don't remember having one single dull night, such was the standard set by the promoters at the Ricky-Tick.

I was there one night when Cream were due on later, so I visited the bar next door with friends, not realising that the man himself – Eric Clapton – was standing right beside me. I regret missing the chance of grabbing a chat with him then before he became known as 'God'.

But in those heady days at one or the other of the Ricky-Tick Clubs, it was the original line ups, the bands as they were first formed who were playing and making history. I recall going into the Ricky-Tick one night and seeing Jimi Hendrix there at the side as we entered, sat at a table, quietly writing something down. But when he hit the stage with his Experience made up of bassist Noel Redding and drummer Mitch Mitchell, the guitar took on a whole new meaning, the quiet man off stage well and truly blew things apart on stage. A night no one there will ever forget – even though we did see him again at other venues later, none could compare with our experience on that night.

BEGINNINGS

It all began in Windsor, upstairs at The Star and Garter pub in Peascod Street, before moving to The Thames Hotel in Barry Avenue near the river, before moving again to Clewer Mead.

Before long, Mansfield and Hayward began reaching out to several other towns in the South such as Guildford, Newbury, Maidenhead, Hounslow, Reading and High Wycombe, and the club moved around reaching new audiences. For a band to get a chance to play at any of the venues they had to be really good – and have something new to offer. The roll call of the bands who played there still fill rock arenas and clubs all over the world today, such was the quality of programming.

In writing about the way the clubs were promoted, musician and songwriter Phillip Goodhand-Tait calls it "the Ricky-Tick Style". He played the Ricky-Tick club circuit many times with his band The Stormsville Shakers, a group formed with Paul Demers on drums, Ivor Shackleton playing guitar, and Kirk Riddle on bass. He says that what distinguished a Ricky-Tick club from any other was firstly the presentation style, their simplistic adverts rolled out by silk screen printing on black posters, with crude white lettering always using a very eye-catching logo that comprised a huge Afro head shouting the blues, stencilled in black or white.

In 1966 in the film *Blow Up*, the club was reconstructed at Elstree Studios for Antonioni, and the director had the Yardbirds playing *Stroll On*, while the film's star David Hemmings looks for co-star Vanessa Redgrave.

Clewer Mead was a large mansion in Windsor, not far from the castle and the River Thames, that became Mansfield and Hayward's headquarters, and the main venue. Windows were covered, walls painted matt black and the task of designing and painting the Afro black blues-shouters in white on either

Re-creation of the Ricky-Tick for the film *Blow Up*, 1966

side of the stage was undertaken by Hogsnort Rupert, in return for living quarters in the boiler room along with the occasional gig for his band.

Another pioneering aspect of the clubs was the introduction to the UK of Motown. It was where artists such as Stevie Wonder played their first gigs in Britain. Other Black blues artists included John Lee Hooker, Jimmy Reed, Sonny Boy Williamson, Lee Dorsey, Don Covay, Rufus Thomas, Arthur Alexander, Solomon Burke and Ben E King. You just have to take a moment to stop and think how many major names in both blues and soul passed through the doors of the Ricky-Tick clubs and met British audiences for the first time to realise the impact these clubs had on British musical culture. Also think what you'd pay today to see these artists, as the entry prices for many gigs back then came in at around fifty pence to a pound! Another unique aspect of the Ricky-Tick Club was the wonderfully named 'Boutick', where you could purchase shirts and other trendy clothes of the day. It was not a place where you would find the band's merchandise like you do now, as there were no T-shirts, nor any singles, albums or other music-related things. That involved a visit to the record store and more than likely a special order, unless it was a single from one of the bigger bands with a well-known record label that you were after.

RICKY-TICK LEGENDS

On a regular night at one of the clubs you could see bands such as Georgie Fame and the Blue Flames, The Alan Price Set, Herbie Goins and his Night-timers, John Mayall and The Bluesbreakers or Zoot Money. During that time, it was the week that the *Hard Road* album came out, I met up with John Mayall's then drummer Aynsley Dunbar, before the set began, and he introduced me to bassist John McVie, and the stunning new guitarist with the band, Peter Green. In fact, I ventured to ask him how he played that long guitar note featured on the 'Supernatural' track, and his answer came, "With me nose!" I left it at that. Yet that pairing became the nucleus for the original line up of Fleetwood Mac. Interestingly, Zoot Money had Andy Summers on guitar then, who went on to fame with The Police within a few more years. Another interesting aside here is that the DJ at our local Stage Club in Oxford went on to join John Mayall for his next album, playing sax, which he often did alongside his DJ duties.

I saw Eric Clapton play under three different line ups: The Yardbirds, making his first appearance at the Star and Garter, Windsor on 22nd October 1963, before playing the Guildford club on 20th December, then back to Windsor for a Yardbirds show on the Christmas Eve. By April 1965, he was back at the Guildford Club with John Mayall as a member of the Bluesbreakers, before another turn back at Windsor in the June of that year. Of course, during his time with the Yardbirds, their debut live album *Five Live Yardbirds* was released.

Clapton had changed bands again before returning to

Windsor in '66, now he was heading for greatness with Cream, alongside Jack Bruce and Ginger Baker, the country's first supergroup, and they played several Ricky-Tick dates before heading off to the USA and the massive stadium venues. Cream played at Windsor 4th September, 1966, September 20th in Bedford, and 23rd saw them at the Newbury Corn Exchange (another Ricky-

Eric Clapton at 6th National Jazz & Blues Festival, Windsor, 1966

THE RICKY-TICK

Geno Washington

Tick Club venue that remained in use for quite a long period). As the New Year came, I was able to catch them again back in Windsor on January 7th. Clapton regularly fills the Royal Albert Hall today but in those early days at the Ricky-Tick Clubs he was honing his skills in front of small live audiences to become one of the greatest guitarists of all time. One set I particularly recall from those opening dates with Cream (in Newbury) left me with a sense of something so exciting, so creative that I felt truly elated. It was no surprise to me that before long they soared above the whole of that early rock/blues scene like no other band. Watching Cream live, they were just so much better than their first album *Fresh Cream*.

Geno Washington *(above)* came over to the UK with the American Air Force, from his hometown in Evansville, Indiana, but stayed and began his career in music in England. He became the lead singer with the superb Ram Jam Band, who were again one hugely popular live band. At each appearance of the band, everyone would be shouting out, "Geno! Geno! Geno!" as he prepared to take the stage. Their debut album, the wonderfully named *Hand Clappin', Foot Stompin', Funky-Butt... Live* album, rose to an amazing No 5 in the album charts. In fact, a few of us were invited to the recording at Piccadilly Studios but I just couldn't make it. The sound of the crowds on that album shows that their mix of soul and funk drew packed venues, covering the big hits of the day from the likes of Otis Redding, Wilson Pickett, Sam and Dave, even to a soul-drenched version of the Rolling Stones' 'Jumping Jack Flash' It wasn't long before the band put out another live album – *Hipsters, Flipsters, Finger Poppin' Daddies*. If it was live, the band were great, but while the studio sessions were fine they lacked the power and fire of the live sets. The Ram Jam Band minus Geno also had themselves a big hit single with 'Black Betty', a song covered many times since, and even for a television advert.

Herbie Goins was another live favourite, and like Geno, he hailed from the USA, but in his case Ocala, in Florida. His father was a Harlem Gospel singer, and like Geno, Herbie came to Britain as part of his military service and he too stayed on. Along with his band The Night-Timers, his early singles sold very well and they were all part of his live set. His biggest hit was 'No One In Your Heart'; others included 'The Incredible Miss Brown'. With his final UK gig just a few years back, he'd retired to live south of Rome, still doing the odd tour when not enjoying his cottage and working in his vineyard. A great live artist who maybe didn't quite get the success he deserved, but in those 60s Ricky-Tick days he was one artist who always put on a great show.

Georgie Fame along with his Blue Flames *(below)* was another singer who opened his recording career with his live set. Though it was recorded at the Flamingo Club it could have just as easily been at Ricky-Tick's, and he later included

drummer Mitch Mitchell in a band featuring some of the best musicians around the country, with his mix of jazz, soul, pop and reggae. Georgie was massively popular not only live but with a string of hit singles, and huge

Georgie Fame & The Blue Flames

THE RICKY-TICK

John Mayall with harmonicas c. 1968

selling albums that still sell well today.

His debut album *Rhythm and Blues at The Flamingo* featured some well-known songs and with the quality of his band Georgie Fame really brought them alive. 'Night Train', 'Let the Good Times Roll', 'Do The Dog', some Mose Allison songs, and his own version of a song very popular at the time 'Baby Please Don't Go' which had been a hit for Them and a Sonny Boy Williamson II original, which was another song that was hugely acclaimed in Georgie's live set. Interestingly, that band included Big Jim Sullivan, one of the most called on session men in the business, who later formed his own band, Tiger, before taking guitar duties on tour with James Last (a very different music altogether, but it paid the rent).

Even John Mayall's debut album was a live one; again, it could have been recorded at any blues club at that time, and a set anyone seeing him at a Ricky-Tick venue would have remembered. His band, in 1964, included Roger Dean on guitar, but not too long afterwards, Roger was replaced by, yes, Eric Clapton, who in reissues did several live recordings with the band that only appeared more recently. Hughie Flint (drums) and John McVie (bass) made up that debut session.

Then there's Zoot Money, who along with his Big Roll Band, appeared at several Ricky-Tick venues. His brand of blues, soul and R&B certainly wowed the crowds who came out, and his own debut release was another live album (*Live at Klooks Kleek*), one that perfectly reflected his live shows. The band was called The All Happening, which summed them up

119

Zoot Money *(left)* and the Big Roll Band

very well, and the album was recorded in 1966. To quote Zoot himself, he says of the band: "We were on full alert." The band included Nick Newell on sax and flute, and Johnny Almond on tenor and baritone sax, who went on to record with other bands (including John Mayall) before settling on the West Coast of the USA. Johnny was only 17 when he joined the band and was barely allowed to drink. Andy Summers was on guitar but in those days he was known as 'Somers'. Colin Allen (drums) and Paul Williams made up the rest of the band. Interestingly, both Colin and Paul returned to the band in 2003, and they had a lot of fun, especially when the band reprised Robert Parker's 'Barefootin', the song that closes the set on that debut live album.

I mentioned earlier a band I only ever saw once: Julian Covey and The Machine, at Newbury's Ricky-Tick Club. They put on one of those never-forgotten sets. A set that's been called

'Super Soul'. The band had a string of pretty good singles, but just didn't quite break through, although their record 'A Little Bit Hurt' became very popular on the Northern Soul scene. Nottingham-born Julian went through too many line-up changes for the band to really settle down to be as good as they were on that night in 1966. The set ended when Julian Covey went to a full drum set alongside the band's then sticksman, Andrew Steele, and produced one fantastic finale – the place was certainly jumping, with a full house. Others that came and went through the various line ups included Jim Cregan (later with Rod Stewart's band), Cliff Barton (keys), Dave Mason (Traffic) and John McVie (bass) who, of course, has been with Fleetwood Mac ever since. Recordings of the band are none too easy to find now, somehow a chance missed, but they made for some great live nights out during those years.

Chris Farlowe is another great vocalist who is still going strong, and still a hugely popular artist, playing all over Europe with several live albums to his name throughout his career. Those early days at both our college balls and Ricky-Tick nights with his Thunderbirds always remain strong in the memory. The band around 1964/5 included Bobby Taylor (guitar), Ricky Charman (bass) Vic Cooper (organ/sax & piano) along with Jimmy Campbell on drums. Again, a band that packed out wherever they played, and Chris himself was known as 'The Voice', probably the best soul-based singer this country has ever produced. Boy, could he sing a song; the strength and power of his voice is exceptional. Today, he has The Norman Beaker Band alongside, but the music is as great and timeless as ever.

There are just so many memories from those Ricky-Tick days (and nights) but one thing will always remain with me, that's just how popular they were. Many of the gigs were packed, everyone having a great time, and the music has never been better than in those days, with the 'Royal family of Windsor' the incredible bands, musicians and artists that filled those stages. Many of the songs we heard are still part of today's

music scene, with more recent bands covering them and adding them to their sets, and guess what? Yes, they sound as great as they ever did, back in those heady, exciting days, when rock, blues and soul filled our ears for the first time. They will never be forgotten. They are timeless classics.

Martin Fuggles *(above)* was the DJ at the Ricky-Tick, Windsor, from 1965 to 1967. He was persuaded to come out of retirement after over 40 years and got back behind the turntables. He is playing the same vinyl for a Ricky-Tick set as in yesteryear.[xiv]

John Mansfield and Philip Hayward's pioneering clubs remain a huge part of our musical heritage, so many thanks to them, because they set something in place in Windsor that developed into those other venues throughout the South of England which gave thousands of young people the chance to see and hear up close all those great bands and musicians who were on their way to worldwide success.

---

i. xiv   see www.rickytick.com

THE RICKY-TICK

A selection of posters from the Ricky-Tick

Sister Rosetta Tharpe performing at the Ricky-Tick Club, Clewer Mead,
Windsor, October 31, 1964.

Fans queueing to get into the Marquee Club

THE MARQUEE CLUB

Charlotte Banks

"Our policy has always been to present the best in pop at reasonable prices, be one step ahead of trends, and foster new talent. We've never been out to make a quick buck and that is the reason we have survived where other clubs have come and gone."

– John Gee

Of all the music venues in London, few can claim more cultural impact than Soho's Marquee Club. In its four decades of life, from 1958 onwards, the small West End club would be instrumental to the rise of prog rock, punk, and even the Mod subculture. If you hung about the area in the latter half of the century, you might have seen Dave Gilmour, hitchhiking from Cambridge to London to see The Who, or bouncers turning away David Bowie and Iggy Pop to a sold-out Human League gig.

The first iteration of the Marquee Club opened in 1958 in the basement of the Academy Cinema in Oxford Street. Its name came from its signature decoration: red-and-white striped backdrop, in the style of a circus tent, designed by legendary theatre photographer Angus McBean. McBean was a real renaissance man: he was a mask-maker, set designer, cult surrealist photographer and portraitist to the stars. He took the photo on the cover of the Beatles' first album, *Please, Please Me.*

It is fitting that the figure behind the Marquee's trademark look had such a creative and varied career.

In late 1957, the basement venue at 165 Oxford Street was struggling to attract a crowd. Throughout the 50s, the space had been used as a ballroom, hosting dance orchestras and big bands. That year, Welsh pianist Dill Jones and his manager Peter Burman started running jazz nights on weekends. However, the British trad jazz scene was losing momentum, and Jones and Burman were struggling to catch the tail wind. These jazz nights were poorly attended, and the two managers were haemorrhaging money. They decided to reach out to jazz's man of the moment: Harold Pendleton.

Born in Southport in 1924, Pendleton's course changed forever when he moved to London in 1948 and struck up a friendship with jazz trombonist Chris Barber. Originally an accountant, he first encountered jazz in London's bars and clubs, and immediately became enchanted with the new sound. A talented entrepreneur, he quickly inserted himself into London's jazz scene as Barber's manager, quitting his accounting job soon after. Tireless and passionate, Pendleton soon rose through the ranks to become the director of the National Jazz Federation (NJF). Pendleton and Barber shared a passion for authentic American blues, and between them would expose UK audiences to greats of the genre, such as Muddy Waters and Howlin' Wolf, despite the antagonism of the protectionist Musician's Union. By 1958, he was organising 200 gigs a year and running *Jazz News*, a weekly magazine. Later that year he would be invited by Lord Montagu to take the reins of the UK's first outdoor jazz festival, held at Beaulieu in Hampshire.

Peter Burman was also involved in the National Jazz Federation. He knocked on Harold Pendleton's door at the NJF offices a few minutes down the road from the Academy Cinema in Carlisle Street. Burman and Jones were struggling to afford the extortionate London rent; Pendleton was looking to acquire a venue to host regular jazz events. After a meeting with George Hoellering, who owned the building, a deal was struck and plans were put in place to launch the new Marquee Club in April.

The first jazz at the Marquee night under Pendleton's management took place on 19 April 1958. *Melody Maker* reported that teen idol Tommy Steele was in attendance at the 'National Jazz Federation's new HQ'. The bill featured the Kenny Baker Half-Dozen (the illustrious jazz trumpeter, not the Star Wars actor) and the Michael Garrick Quartet.

Over the course of the next few years, the weekend jazz nights started to pick up momentum. A Friday night was added. Pendleton's star was beginning to rise alongside that of the club. In 1961, he organised the National Jazz Festival, in a small, red-and-white marquee. The festival took place at Richmond Athletic Ground over the last weekend of August, creating a permanent fixture in the August bank holiday spot. The line-up included Johnny Dankworth, Chris Barber's band, Dick Charlesworth and His City Gents, and Tubby Hayes. The festival would be run by Marquee productions until 1988, although it changed its name to match its new location in 1971,

Harold and Barbara Pendleton, Marquee Club, Wardour St, 1983

when it moved to Reading.

1962 would be a defining year for the club. Reflecting the current vogue amongst musicians, Pendleton started Rhythm and Blues nights on Wednesdays and Fridays. On the 10th May 1962, Alexis Korner's Blues Incorporated started a Thursday residency. A young Eric Clapton was in the crowd on that first night. When he went home, he asked his parents to buy him an electric guitar.

THE ROLLING STONES

In July 1962, Pendleton was faced with a run-of-the-mill logistical challenge. Alexis Korner's Blues Incorporated could not make their usual Thursday slot, because they had been invited on to BBC Radio's Jazz Club.

18-year-old Mick Jagger, who was at the time a finance and accounting student at the London School of Economics (LSE), and sometimes sang with Blues Incorporated (although hadn't been invited to the BBC), asked Pendleton if his new musical project could replace them for the evening.

Jagger had recently reconnected with childhood friend Keith Richards, and they bonded over American blues and rock 'n' roll. After jamming with Blues Incorporated for a while, they responded to an advert that Brian Jones had put in *Jazz News*, looking for bandmates. They had been jamming together for just over a month when Jagger managed to land them their first gig.

As legend has it, Jones, on the phone to a journalist, was struggling to come up with a name for his new rhythm and blues outfit when his eyes rested on the back of a Muddy Waters LP that was lying around. *Jazz News* carried an item advertising that on 12 July 1962, the Rollin' Stones would play their debut gig on the Marquee's red-and-white striped stage.

On that night in July, Mick Jagger, Brian Jones, Keith Richards, Ian Stewart, Dick Taylor and Tony Chapman or Mick

The Rolling Stones with Ian Stewart

Avory (according to different accounts) took to the stage for the first time under their new name. Using equipment rented with money borrowed from Jagger's dad, they played covers of Chuck Berry, Jimmy Reed and Elmore James. In a year's time they had added a permanent drummer, Charlie Watts, and a 'g' to the end of their name.

If attendance at the gig would become bragging rights soon after, you might not have known it at the time. In his autobiography, Bill Wyman recalled a rocky start to the Stones' live career. Keith Richards disliked the early Marquee crowds, believing that the jazz audiences were not receptive to the Stones' heavier sounds. It would take a while before they would live the glamorous rockstar life. Jagger, Jones and Richards were living together in a dank apartment in Chelsea, Jones unable to hold down a job. Richards even got kicked out of the Marquee that year for starting a fight with a bouncer.

The Stones may have only been paid £10 a gig in those early days at the Marquee, but their time at the venue not only served to kick-start their career, but put them in touch with one of their long-term collaborators. The Stones met pianist Nicky Hopkins on their 10 January 1963 gig, when they were still second on the bill to Cyril Davies. Hopkins would provide the piano on some of their most iconic tracks and contribute his unique sound to recordings by other big names of the 60s – the Kinks, The Who, and the Beatles.

Although the Stones moved on from the Marquee to residencies at the Crawdaddy and Eel Pie Island hotel, they didn't completely cut ties. A Rolling Stones gig on 12 March 1971 had Keith Richards turning up to the venue barefoot and two hours late, parking his Bentley on a double yellow line and swinging his guitar at Harold Pendleton's head. The group also returned to the location for a 50th anniversary photo.

WARDOUR STREET

While the Rolling Stones were still finding their feet, the Marquee's owners were having more success supporting the wider movement. There were two important rhythm and blues residencies in 1963: Mann-Hugg (later known as Manfred Mann) and John Mayall and the Bluesbreakers.

However, by the end of 1963, the club's fortunes were beginning to turn. The jazz scene was slowly ebbing away. Attempts to revive it fell flat. Pendleton's new jazz and poetry nights were poorly attended. Another huge blow was the sudden death of Blues Incorporated's vocalist and harmonica player, Cyril Davies, on 7 January 1964.

Towards the end of 1963, Pendleton was given six months' notice to move out. The owners of the Academy Cinema wanted to use the basement to open another auditorium. The Academy Cinema eventually closed in 1986 and the address is now occupied by Flannels' flagship store, selling designer clothing to wealthy tourists.

The last night at the Marquee's original location featured jazz saxophonist Stan Getz and the Yardbirds, fresh from signing to EMI's Columbia label. At the time, the Yardbirds' lead guitarist was Eric Clapton.

On 13 March 1964, the club moved a few minutes down the road to its most iconic location at 90 Wardour Street. The new club kept the original red-and-white circus-like decoration. Leaning into its reputation as an innovator, the layout differed significantly from standard live jazz presentation at the time, with carpeted floors and large mirror panels placed around the room to create the feeling of space.

The first night at the new venue had both Eric Clapton (with the Yardbirds) and Rod Stewart gracing the stage, as the latter accompanied Long John Baldry and the Hoochie Coochie Men. Also on the bill was American Blues harmonica player Sonny Boy Williamson.

Instrumental in the Marquee's trailblazing role in the 60s was secretary-turned-manager John Gee. Gee was a serious figure, impeccably-dressed and well-spoken. He told *Melody Maker:*

Steampacket: Rod Stewart, Long John Baldry, Julie Driscoll & Brian Auger

"We always make it clear that the Marquee is not a place to doss down for the night. Nor is it a place to have a snog in the dark or buy pot." He was passionate about jazz and idolised the American greats – Frank Sinatra, Ella Fitzgerald, Louis Armstrong – but was always looking for the Next Big Thing.

He scored an early hit when he booked a group called the High Numbers, presented to him by managers Kit Lambert and Chris Stamp. Within weeks they were packing out the venue. They soon changed their name to The Who and started a 7-week Thursday residency at the Marquee on the 24th November 1964. They would maintain a better relationship with the Marquee club over the years than the Stones, headlining its 10th anniversary event in 1968.

In 1966, *Melody Maker* advertised a way-out 'Giant Mystery Happening' taking place at the Marquee, with musicians Pete Townshend, Keith Roe, Cornelius Cardew, Graham Bond, Ginger Baker, Mike Taylor, and David Izenzon. Happenings, one-off live art events, were popular with avant-garde artists in the 60s such as Allan Kaprow and Claes Oldenburg. The 'Giant Mystery Happening' was not reviewed kindly by one *Melody Maker* journalist, who was not impressed by "some substandard

The Who at the Marquee in May 1965. Photo: Bob Baker

beat music" and "a sort of knockabout poetry set which contained some of the most inane lines of blank verse ever heard outside of a kindergarten". However, more happenings followed soon after. It was at the third such happening that Syd Barrett, Roger Waters, Rick Wright and Nick Mason stepped up to the slot, appearing on the bill as the 'Trip'.

The Marquee was where, also in 1966, Ken Pitt, enchanted by the 19-year-old David Jones singing Rodgers and Hammerstein's 'You'll Never Walk Alone,' offered him a place to stay. He encouraged him to change his name, to avoid confusion with actor (and later Monkees member) Davy Jones. The singer would later adopt the name Bowie.

In 1968, the Marquee Club advertised the return of a 'Marquee group'. The Yardbirds, having undergone a few iterations, were returning for their first London gig with a new line-up. The 'New Yardbirds' had the lineup of Jimmy Page, Robert Plant, John Paul Jones and John Bonham. The handbill boasted that Jimmy Page was now playing a 'specially built Fender 6 pedal steel guitar' as well as his usual guitar. Hounslow-born Jimmy Page was no stranger to the Marquee, having practised his craft through jam sessions there with bands such as Alexis Korner's Blues Incorporated, which led him to be approached as a session player for recording. He would later appear on records for the Kinks, The Who and Van Morrison.

The Marquee would later be at the centre of another movement: punk. The Sex Pistols played the club on 12 February 1976, as they were starting to transition from art school venues, supporting pub rockers Eddie and the Hot Rods. They walked offstage, sat with the audience, upset chairs and smashed the main act's gear. Punk fashion pioneer Pamela Rooke, better known as 'Jordan' or 'Jordan Mooney', was in attendance, getting thrown across the dance floor. Pete Shelley of the Buzzcocks would be inspired to start a band after reading the review of the concert in the *NME*, in which Steve Jones told a journalist: "Actually we're not into music. We're into chaos."

Jimi Hendrix at the Marquee, 1967

Not only did the Marquee provide the training ground for future superstars, Pendleton used the venue to carry on his work in bringing big international acts to London audiences. On the Sunday before July 16 1966, Simon and Garfunkel played their only London appearance. On 2 March 1967 the Jimi Hendrix Experience chose the iconic red-and-white backdrop for a performance on the German TV show Beat Club, performing tracks now recognised as classics of the rock canon, 'Hey Joe' and 'Purple Haze'.

In its Wardour Street era, bands used the unique acoustics of the room to record live tracks for release. On 20th March 1964, the Yardbirds recorded 10 live tracks – covers of American blues and R&B artists such as Chuck Berry, Bo Diddley and Howlin' Wolf – which were released at the end of the year as an album called *Five Live Yardbirds*. Although it failed to chart at the time, it is now considered a classic snapshot of the British blues mania. Decades later, Iron Maiden and Guns 'n' Roses would also release tracks recorded within the Marquee's red-and-white striped walls.

Management went even further in 1966, opening a recording studio with a four-track mixing desk on the upper floor. Marquee Studios, under the management of Spencer Brooks, would be used by Elton John, Marillion, Vangelis, the

Clash, Elliot Murphy, Daevid Allen, the Penny Peeps, Ralph McTell and Graham Bonnet.

For a club that didn't have an alcohol licence until 1970, both artists and punters knew how to have a good time. On the 24th November 1966, at least twenty policemen and five firemen cleared the club after the Move let off several fireworks and smashed up a TV set with an axe. They were banned for five months. This didn't sour their relationship too much – the Move would later record all the tracks for Britain's first 33.3 rpm pop EP in 1968 at the Marquee Club. The Moody Blues, who had their greatest hit with 'Nights in White Satin', once sent out invitations for a Marquee gig to the music press via homing pigeon.

A pre-Stevie-Nicks Fleetwood Mac also frequented the Marquee early in their career. Mick Fleetwood would attach a large rubber dildo to a kick drum, wobbling around as his foot hit the pedals. The dildo's name was Harold.

END OF THE ROAD

Twenty years of thunderous volume had taken a toll on the building. In 1987, a commission determined that the building's facade had slipped towards the pavement by an unacceptable amount, and had to be demolished in the interest of safety. After almost a quarter of a century in Wardour Street, the Marquee club, and with it, Marquee Studios, were to close.

The last night at Wardour Street took place on 18th July 1988, and featured Joe Satriani. Harold Pendleton sold the club to Billy Gaff. The site is now occupied by a bar and restaurant called, confusingly, 100 Wardour St. The venue still hosts live music and DJ sets, although you're more likely to hear Crystal Waters than Muddy Waters.

Gaff opened the Marquee's largest iteration yet, at 105 Charing Cross Road, a 5-minute walk from Wardour Street. It failed to live up to its legend. The biggest crowd the new venue managed to draw was for a tribute act for The Jam, somewhat embarrassingly for a club that made its name championing new trends in music. The club lasted less than ten years and is now a branch of Wetherspoons.

The next attempt at carrying on the Marquee's legacy took the project even further from its roots. The Marquee N1, run by a group of entrepreneurs including Eurythmics' Dave Stewart, lasted for a year before running into financial difficulties. It was then taken over by the Academy Music Group and reopened at the O2 Academy Islington, where it has hosted some of the biggest names in 21st century pop and rock, such as The Script, Paramore, and My Chemical Romance.

One last-ditch attempt to revive the brand was equally ill-fated. Under the management of Nathan Lowry, the Marquee Club moved back to Soho, a short walk from its previous locations, at 1 Leicester Square. In another nod to the past, the new venue's opening night provided a platform for a handful of unsigned artists. The club was forced to close in 2007 after they got into licensing issues with Westminster Council. The club continued for a short time as a pop-up in St Martins Lane in Covent Garden before closing for good on 10th February 2008. The last band to play under the Marquee name was Torn Asunder, a short-lived 'old school rock' band from Colchester.

In its almost exactly fifty year existence, the Marquee Club played a part in nearly every development in British popular music, but it started with a love of jazz and a team of adventurous music-lovers tirelessly searching for the future of music.

Exterior, The Marquee Bar and Club on Upper St Martins Lane in Covent Garden in London, 2007. Photo: Kiwi

Girl punks in the bathroom at the 100 Club, 1981
Photo: Helma Hellinga

THE 100 CLUB

Richard Luck

"The 100 Club is the worst place to play in for acoustics in the world. It is evil and unpleasant on the stage. I can listen to bands there and from the back it sounds alright. On the stage, it feels like hell."

– Chris Barber

It's rather fitting that we begin with a quote concerning noise and the 100 Club since, in the venue's most celebrated incarnation, there was one helluva racket going on.

The focal point for the period in question was the 100 Club Punk Special which took place between Monday September 20th and Tuesday September 21st 1976. Why these days rather than a weekend? Because those dates had been given over to, among other things, the venue's regular trad. jazz Sunday session. Not that the slightly unusual schedule put off the major acts of the time. On the contrary, Monday's barnstormer comprised an opening set from Subway Sect, a largely-improvised performance by Suzie(sic) And The Banshees (complete with the lead singer reciting The Lord's Prayer), plus twin headliners in the shape of The Clash and the Sex Pistols.

The following day, it fell to French punk pioneers Stinky Toys to jerk the curtain prior to Chris Spedding taking to the stage with the very green Vibrators. The festival was then brought to a close by Bolton's Buzzcocks, whose performance was slightly overshadowed by the preceding set from Croydon's The Damned, during which then Banshees drummer Sid Vicious, threw a pint glass, the shards from which blinded an audience member.

Such violent delights would've been the furthest thing from Robert Feldman's mind when he hired out what was then Macks Restaurant – address 100 Oxford Street – for an evening of jazz on Sunday 24th October, 1942. A big hit from the off with visiting GIs, these Feldman Swing Club shindigs ran throughout the remainder of the war into the 1950s, attracting a who's who of household names.

Glenn Miller, Benny Goodman, John Dankworth, Louis Armstrong, Ray Ellington, Humphrey Lyttleton – by the time the 100 Club became so known in 1964, when Roger Horton took the helm, it was the Ronnie Scott's of its day: oh, and yes, Ronnie Scott was a 100 Club regular, too.

Then rock 'n' roll arrived and jazz was very much yesterday's music – the Kinks, the Stones, The Who – were just three of the biggest British acts of the 1960s for whom the 100 Club would become something of a home from home. A residence

Chris Barber

at the venue wasn't just a feather in the cap; the club was the perfect place to experience playing in circumstances that were at best cozy and at worst claustrophobic. If you went down a storm at the 100 Club, the cheers could be deafening. If you had an off-night, you didn't just hear each individual catcall; there was a good chance you might cop a spot of the pissed-off punter's saliva into the bargain.

It wasn't just the huge blues-influence bands of the day that played the 100 Club, mind you. Aforementioned jazz/blues legend Chris Barber, mightn't have been a fan of the venue's acoustics but that didn't deter him from bringing the mighty Muddy Waters to Oxford Street. BB King and Howlin' Wolf also took to the stage at the 100 Club, their band numbers sometimes swollen by the likes of Keith Richards who, though a bona fide rock star, was first and foremost a devotee of the blues.

Dave Peabody, musician and photographer recalls:

"Two legendary bluesmen, Johnny Shines and Robert Lockwood Jr., both of whom had shared experience with the even more legendary Robert Johnson, were playing as a duo at the 100 Club back in 1979. I had previously met Johnny Shines in Oslo, Norway when we were both gigging, and I had invited him out for a meal. The easy going Mr. Shines was the polar opposite of the perpetually grumpy Mr. Lockwood. At the 100 Club, Johnny cordially invited me to the dressing room to introduce me to Robert Jr., telling him that I also played the blues. This information was like a red rag to a bull. With one hand Robert pinned me to the wall, jabbing me in the chest with one on his long bony fingers, while yelling in my face … 'It's white boys like you that's stealin' MY music!' Looking over Robert's shoulder I saw Johnny doubled up with laughter. I realised, much to my relief, I'd live to tell the tale. Johnny told Robert to leave me be… and the two of them left the dressing room to go play a set of wonderful blues."

L-R: Johnny Shines, Robert Lockwood Jr., 100 Club, 1979. Photo: Dave Peabody

By the end of the 70s, the 100 Club's blues-rock era gave way to what became known as punk. Overseen in large part by Brewers Droop lead singer Ron Watts, the venue hosted punk acts from either side of the Atlantic. All of which said, not every band booked felt as vital or admirable as Angelic Upstarts and Black Flag: these avowed anti-fascist acts might have raised more than an objection had they known that the club's stage would later accommodate far-right Oi! outfits as well as the later, white supremacist incarnation of Skrewdriver.

It couldn't last, of course. As surely as punk mutated into New Wave, so the 100 Club's title as alternative music titan would be taken up by places like The Blitz. It was still capable of staging the odd coup mind you, the most significant of which involved one of the venue's 60s regular fixtures.

For it was in 1982 that the Rolling Stones rocked back up to the 100 Club to play a warm-up gig ahead of a European tour. An evening that yielded no end of photos of Mick prancing about with his top off, the experience proved so enjoyable that the boys returned again in 1986, this time to perform a tribute concert for their late pianist Ian Stewart.

And all the while, the 100 Club continued to hold weekly Trad. jazz evenings (owner Roger Horton's music-of-choice), together with regular Northern Soul all-nighters and – at the height of the anti-apartheid movement – ANC benefit gigs. To this day the club's décor reeks of its punk heyday but the venue's bill of fare has always reflected its significance as a home to music of many stripes.

Throughout much of the 100 Club's existence there have been stories about if and when it's going to close. The most recent of these broke in 2010 with a press release explaining that the venue's losses were so great, it would have to close for business come the end of the year.

There followed a rescue mission that, among many other things, underlined just how important blues and rock have been to the venue and its storied history. The Save The 100 Club Benefit Concert was the brainchild of American guitarist Stephen Dale Petit, the busker-turned-university music lecturer.

Ronnie Wood performing at the 2010 benefit gig for the 100 Club

Having collaborated with seemingly everyone who was anyone, Petit was able to assemble a crack blues-rock outfit comprising Ronnie Wood, Mick Taylor, original Stones bassist Dick Taylor and – who else? – Chris Barber.

Described by *The Times'* music writer David Sinclair as a gig "worthy of a place in the 100 Club folklore", the benefit concert also brought fresh attention to the venue's very real plight.

"I'm very concerned about the 100 Club," Ray Davies explained to *Spinner*. "The Kinks played there a lot... it's such an iconic venue... we shouldn't allow things like that to close down. Everything is being overrun by the chain stores and the conglomerates and it's such a pity that the 100 Club has to suffer like that."

Davies also had a clear idea who should put their hands in their pockets to save the club from closure: "Simon Cowell should underwrite the money needed to save the 100 Club. That would be a real payback – the amount of money he takes out of pop music he could put some back in."

Fortunately, the benefit gig kept both Simon Cowell and the wolf from the door; the money raising sufficient funds to keep the venue going while current owner Jeff Horton – yes the son of Roger – secured the club's future through a sponsorship deal with Converse.

If being bankrolled by a subsidiary of Nike doesn't sound particularly punk rock, a more recent hook up with Fred Perry makes a little more sense what with the clothing label being synonymous with the music and subculture of the 1960s and 70s. Then again, if the whole business of naming rights full stop isn't very punk then it's probably worth pointing out once more that neither was the 100 Club, at least for the vast majority of its eight decades as a music venue.

According to promoter Jim Driver, punk rock, for example, was only accommodated by the club because people were willing to pay to lay on gigs there. By all accounts, Roger Horton had far more time for Kenny Ball than for Joe Strummer, for Chris

Barber than for Captain Sensible. It was hard cash rather than a commitment to new music that led the venue to embrace what many thought unembraceable.

And besides, if outside assistance means that the Oxford Street fixture has a half-way decent chance of getting to celebrate its centenary, it seems a small price to pay. Whether or not the claims about the 100 Club being the longest running music venue in Britain/Europe/the solar system (delete according to whom you believe) are true, were a certain Oxford Street basement to fall silent, it really would be like punk never happened. Or blues-rock for that matter.

Exterior 100 Club, at 100 Oxford Street, Soho

Long John Baldry by the River Thames c. 1964

Biographies

CHARLOTTE BANKS

Charlotte studied PPE at Oxford and is currently training for an NCTJ with News Associates. She is a freelance music journalist who has written for *Nightshift* and *Oxfordshire Music Scene*, and is currently writing for *South West Londoner*.

PETE CLACK

Pete grew up in Oxfordshire, playing in bands and visiting clubs. He worked on research in Physics and Chemistry at the University of Oxford. He has written for both motor club and youth magazines, and now writes for *Blues In Britain*, also *The Dub*, a roots reggae magazine. He lives on the edge of the

Cotswolds with his wife Pauline, has two grown up children, and is still writing songs and performing in bands.

PETE FEENSTRA

Since the 70s, Pete has been promoting music and contributing to *Classic Rock Blues* magazine. He wrote the book accompanying the Family 'Once Upon A Time' boxed set and is also features editor for *Get Ready to ROCK!* In 2016, he won two Lifetime Achievement Awards for his services to the blues. In 2019, he won Best Radio Show, and in 2020 he was voted UK Blues Broadcaster of the Year at the UK Blues Awards. In 2022 he was voted 'Best Podcast' in the Wrinkly Rockers Club 2021 Awards.

ROBERT HOKUM

Robert Hokum is the alter-ego of Bob Salmons who has had careers in the Music Industry, National Newspapers and Market Research, being involved in events such as Rock against Racism, the rise of Punk, the fall of Fleet Street and the development of the Internet. He is best known as the founder of the Ealing Blues Festival and as a Director of The Ealing Club Community Interest Company. Born and raised in Ealing, he now lives in Twickenham with his wife and two daughters.

PATRICK HUMPHRIES

Patrick began writing as a "hip young gunslinger" on *NME* back in the last century. Since then he has contributed to *The Times, The Observer, The Guardian, Vox, Mojo* and *Record Collector* as well as broadcasting on BBC Radio 1, 2, 4 and 6 Music. He is the author of over 20 books, including the first-ever biography of Nick Drake; the authorised biography of Richard Thompson and most recently, *Rolling Stones 69*.

RICHARD LUCK

Richard is a feature writer, critic and author. A regular contributor to *The New European*, he also writes or has written for *Empire, FourFourTwo, Film4.com, Rolling Stone, Neon, Uncut, GQ* and *Total Film*. His books include profiles of Sam Peckinpah,

Steve McQueen and the Madchester music scene. Twitter: @RMGLUCK2017.

CHERYL ROBSON

Cheryl is an award-winning writer, editor and filmmaker. Her multi-award-winning documentary *Rock 'n' Roll Island; Where Legends Were Born* tells the history of the Eel Pie Island Hotel and SW London music scene. It was a *Sunday Times* Critics' Choice and *Radio Times'* Pick of the Week when broadcast by BBC4, 2020. Cheryl commissioned and edited *50 Women in the Blues,* featuring music photos by Jennifer Noble and writing by Zoe Howe. She is translating and editing *Pop Rock Icons* by top French music writer Philippe Margotin. www.cherylrobson.net

DAVID SINCLAIR

David has been a musician since the 70s and a music journalist since the 80s. As chief rock/pop correspondent of *The Times of London* and a contributor to *Rolling Stone, Billboard, Q* magazine and many others, he was fortunate to see and meet many of the bands and stars who came up through the London gig circuit. As a singer, songwriter and bandleader of David Sinclair Four (DS4), he has been privileged to have played at many of these venues himself. The new DS4 album, *Apropos Blues,* launches at the Half Moon, September 2022. www.davidsinclairfour.com

GINA WAY

Gina and her husband Warren have been producing and promoting live music events since 1998. For over 20 years she produced dance and musical theatre events (under the label Aspects of Dance) for charity, including two Royal Galas at Richmond Theatre. She has been running the Eel Pie Club since 2000. Gina was a regular visitor to The Eel Pie Island Jazz Club in the 1960s (when still at school) and is a contributor to *The British Beat Explosion* book. www.eelpieclub.com

Connie Lush performs at the Eel Pie Club, Twickenham
Photo: Jennifer Noble

ALISTAIR YOUNG

Alistair was born just as the Rolling Stones were launching *Let It Bleed* and the Beatles were coming to an end. Music was always his first interest but a career in medical sales/publishing pushed that aside for a while.

Ronnie Wood's biography first sparked his interest in Ealing's Music heritage and this has been followed by library visits, emails and conversations with people who lived through the days of the club. By setting up a community interest company, assuring backing from The Arts Council and co-producing the definitive film about the club, he hopes the legacy of the Ealing Club can live beyond the history books.

Manfred Mann, London, 1966
L-R: Manfred Mann, Klaus Voorman, Mike D'Abo, Mike Hugg

More great books on Music

50 Women in the Blues
Jennifer Noble
Zoë Howe
9781913641191
£19.99

The British Beat Explosion:
Rock 'n' Roll Island
Ed. JC Wheatley
9781906582470
£9.99

Women Make Noise: Girl Bands from
Motown to the Modern
Ed. Julia Downes
9780956632913
£15.99

On the Trail of Americana Music
Ralph Brookfield
9781913641092
£15.99